*Love Letters
of Great Men*

Love Letters of Great Men

Edited by Ursula Doyle

St. Martin's Press ♏ New York

LOVE LETTERS OF GREAT MEN. This selection and commentary copyright © 2008 by
Ursula Doyle. All rights reserved. Printed in the United States of America. For
information, address St. Martin's Press, 175 Fifth Avenue, New York, N.Y. 10010.

www.stmartins.com

Library of Congress Cataloging-in-Publication Data

Love letters of great men / edited by Ursula Doyle.—1st U.S. ed.
    144 p. cm.
    Includes bibliographical references.
    ISBN-13: 978-0-312-56744-6
    ISBN-10: 0-312-56744-8
    1. Love-letters. I. Doyle, Ursula.
PN6140.L7L63 2008
809.6'93543—dc22

                                                          2008035392

First published in Great Britain by Macmillan, an imprint of Pan Macmillan Ltd

First U.S. Edition: December 2008

        10 9 8 7 6 5 4 3 2 1

To the memory of three great men:
JSS, JD, AJD

Contents

Introduction   1

Pliny the Younger to his wife, Calpurnia   5

King Henry VIII to Anne Boleyn   8

William Congreve to Mrs Arabella Hunt   9

Richard Steele to Miss Mary Scurlock   13

George Farquhar to Anne Oldfield   16

Alexander Pope to Martha Blount   19

Alexander Pope to Teresa Blount   20

Alexander Pope to Lady Mary Wortley Montagu   21

David Hume to Madame de Boufflers   23

Laurence Sterne to Catherine Fourmantel   26

Laurence Sterne to Lady Percy   27

Denis Diderot to Sophie Volland   30

Henry Frederick, Duke of Cumberland, to Lady Grosvenor   32

Wolfgang Amadeus Mozart to his wife, Constanze   36

Lord Nelson to Lady Emma Hamilton   40

Robert Burns to Mrs Agnes Maclehose   43

*Johann Christoph Friedrich von Schiller to
    Charlotte von Lengefeld*   45

Napoléon Bonaparte to his wife, Josephine   49

Daniel Webster to Josephine Seaton   54

Ludwig van Beethoven to his 'Immortal Beloved'   57

William Hazlitt to Sarah Walker   61

Lord Byron to Lady Caroline Lamb   65

Lord Byron to the Countess Guiccioli   67

John Keats to Fanny Brawne   69

Honoré de Balzac to the Countess Ewelina Hanska   76

Victor Hugo to Adèle Foucher   80

Nathaniel Hawthorne to his wife, Sophia   84

Benjamin Disraeli to Mary Anne Wyndham Lewis   87

Charles Darwin to Emma Wedgwood   94

Alfred de Musset to George Sand   98

Robert Schumann to Clara Wieck   101

Robert Browning to Elizabeth Barrett   105

Gustave Flaubert to Louise Colet   109

Gustave Flaubert to George Sand   109

Walter Bagehot to Elizabeth Wilson   112

Mark Twain to Olivia Langdon   117

William F. Testerman to Miss Jane Davis   120

Charles Stewart Parnell to Katharine O'Shea   123

Oscar Wilde to Lord Alfred Douglas   126

Pierre Curie to Marie Sklodovska (Marie Curie)   131

G. K. Chesterton to Frances Blogg   135

Captain Alfred Bland to his wife, Violet   138

Regimental Sergeant-Major James Milne to his wife, Meg   141

Second Lieutenant John Lindsay Rapoport to his fiancée   142

Bibliography   147

Acknowledgements   149

A note on the type   151

Introduction

The commonly held view these days is that people don't write love letters any more, and that email and text messaging are death to romance. And it does seem unlikely that even the most impassioned lover would today claim, as the playwright Congreve does, that 'nothing but you can lay hold of my mind, and that can lay hold of nothing but you'; then again, Congreve was a literary genius. But Nelson most definitely was not, and even he came up with the stirring formulation, to Lady Hamilton, 'Nelson's Alpha and Omega is Emma!' Perhaps people have grown less romantic and more cynical. Or perhaps people were less self-conscious than we are today; certainly, irony, the presiding spirit of our age, has almost no place in this collection.

So, while reading all these love letters, and finding out the stories behind them, it was tempting to think that we modern barbarians have lost faith, both in love itself and in the art of its expression. But in fact, for the most part, it wasn't the elegantly worked, impassioned declarations that I found most touching in the letters that follow, or rather, not those alone; it was when they bumped up against more prosaic concerns, like the unreliability of the postal service, or the need for clean linen, or the sending of regards to the beloved's mother, or a description of a dream, that the letters suddenly came alive somehow, and their writers seemed more human. It could be argued that the flowery declarations were more for show (and, in some cases, posterity) than the genuine expression of genuine feeling – that they grew from convention rather than conviction. And there is a case for calling this book, 'Great Men: Going On About Themselves Since AD 61' – certainly some of those here would have benefited from being taken aside and gently told: it's not All About You.

But to claim that a text message saying IN PUB FTBL XTR TIME BACK LATR XX is more genuine, and therefore romantic, than a declaration such as Byron's that 'I more than love you and cannot cease to love you' is obviously nonsense. So while it is to be hoped that this collection entertains, moves and sometimes amuses its readers, it might also serve to remind today's Great Men that literary genius is not a requirement for a heartfelt letter – or text message, or email – of love.

Ursula Doyle, London, 2008

John Donne
Anne Donne
Un-done

John Donne writing from Fleet Prison to his wife
after their secret wedding, December 1601

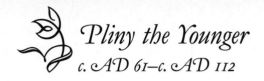

Pliny the Younger
c. AD 61–c. AD 112

Pliny the Younger (Gaius Plinius Caecilius Secundus) was the son of a landowner in northern Italy. After the death of his father, he was brought up by his uncle, Pliny the Elder, the author of a famous ency-clopaedia on natural history. In AD 79, Pliny the Elder was killed during the eruption of Vesuvius.

Pliny had a career in law and government, first as a consul, and then as governor of a Roman province. He left behind ten books of letters: nine to friends and colleagues, the tenth to the emperor Trajan.

To Calpurnia, his wife

You will not believe what a longing for you possesses me. The chief cause of this is my love; and then we have not grown used to be apart. So it comes to pass that I lie awake a great part of the night, thinking of you; and that by day, when the hours return at which I was wont to visit you, my feet take me, as it is so truly said, to your chamber, but not finding you there I return, sick and sad at heart, like an excluded lover. The only time that is free from these torments is when I am being worn out at the bar, and in the suits of my friends. Judge you what must be my life when I find my repose in toil, my solace in wretchedness and anxiety. Farewell.

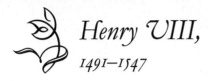

Henry VIII,
1491–1547

Henry VIII first encountered Anne Boleyn in 1526, when he was married to his first wife, Katherine of Aragon. The Roman Catholic Church did not allow divorce, and so Henry, obsessed with Anne, who refused to become his mistress, moved heaven and earth to persuade the Pope to grant him an annulment. The Pope refused, which led to Henry's break with Rome and the establishment of the Church of England with Henry as its Supreme Head (Henry did not have problems with self-esteem: see the kind gift to Anne he mentions in the letter below). The couple were finally married, after seven years of turmoil, in January 1533, and Anne gave birth to her daughter Elizabeth (who became Elizabeth I) that September. In May 1536, Queen Anne was arrested and charged with adultery with several men including her own brother, George, Viscount Rochford. She was found guilty, and beheaded at the Tower of London. On the same day, her marriage to Henry was declared null and void. Eleven days later, Henry married Jane Seymour, the only one of the lucky six wives to bear him a son who survived him, Edward VI.

To Anne Boleyn

My Mistress and my Friend:

My heart and I surrender themselves into your hands, and we supplicate to be commended to your good graces, and that by absence your affections may not be diminished to us, for that would be to augment our pain, which would be a great pity, since absence gives enough, and more than I ever thought could be felt. This brings to my mind a fact in astronomy, which is, that the further the poles are from the sun, notwithstanding, the more scorching is the heat. Thus is it with our love; absence has placed distance between us, nevertheless fervor increases – at least on my part. I hope the same from you, assuring you that in my case the anguish of absence is so great that it would be intolerable were it not for the firm hope I have of your indissoluble affection towards me. In order to remind you of it, and because I cannot in person be in your presence, I send you the thing which comes nearest that is possible, that is to say, my picture, and the whole device, which you already know of, set in bracelets, wishing myself in their place when it pleases you. This is from the hand of

Your servant and friend,

H.R.

William Congreve
1670–1729

William Congreve was a celebrated dramatist, best known for his play *The Way of the World*; Arabella Hunt was a musician at Court and a favourite of Queen Mary. Arabella was married in 1680 to one James Howard; she filed for an annulment six months later on the not-unreasonable grounds that James was actually a cross-dressing widow called Amy Poulter. Unsurprisingly, Arabella never married again ('Mrs' was at this time an honorary form of address for a woman out of her teens). Congreve also remained unmarried, but had longstanding love affairs with Anna Bracegirdle, an actress for whom he wrote a number of parts, and Henrietta, Duchess of Marlborough, with whom he had a daughter in 1723.

To Mrs Arabella Hunt

Dear Madam

– Not believe that I love you? You cannot pretend to be so incredulous. If you do not believe my tongue, consult my eyes, consult your own. You will find by yours that they have charms; by mine that I have a heart which feels them. Recall to mind what happened last night. That at least was a lover's kiss. Its eagerness, its fierceness, its warmth, expressed the god its parent. But oh! Its sweetness, and its melting softness expressed him more. With trembling in my limbs, and fevers in my soul, I ravish'd it. Convulsions, pantings, murmurings shew'd the mighty disorder within me: the mighty disorder increased by it. For those dear lips shot through my heart, and thro' my bleeding vitals, delicious poison, and an avoidless but yet a charming ruin.

What cannot a day produce? The night before I thought myself a happy man, in want of nothing, and in fairest expectation of fortune; approved of by men of wit, and applauded by others. Pleased, nay charmed with my friends, my then dearest friends, sensible of every delicate pleasure, and in their turns possessing all.

But Love, almighty Love, seems in a moment to have removed me to a prodigious distance from every object but you alone. In the midst of crowds I remain in solitude. Nothing but you can lay hold of my mind, and that can lay hold of nothing but you. I appear transported to some foreign desert with you (oh, that I were really thus transported!), where, abundantly supplied with everything, in thee, I might live out an age of uninterrupted ecstasy.

The scene of the world's great stage seems suddenly and sadly chang'd. Unlovely objects are all around me, excepting thee; the charms of all the world appear to be translated to thee. Thus in this sad, but oh, too pleasing state! my soul can fix upon nothing but thee; thee it contemplates, admires, adores, nay depends on, trusts on you alone.

If you and hope forsake it, despair and endless misery attend it.

Richard Steele
1672–1729

Richard Steele was a journalist, writer and politician, who with his friend Joseph Addison founded the *Spectator* magazine. Mary Scurlock was his second wife; he met her at the funeral of his first, and courted her with a single-minded passion. The second letter here, written two weeks before their wedding, is both amusing and touching in Steele's description of himself as a man completely distracted from day-to-day concerns by thoughts of his beloved. Richard and Mary were married in 1707, although their marriage remained secret for some time after that, perhaps for reasons of propriety – this could explain the rather mundane postscript to the third letter below. Their marriage was famously happy, although sometimes tempestuous, and she remained throughout his life his 'dear Prue'. Steele wrote his wife more than four hundred letters both before and during their marriage; she died in 1718.

To Mary Scurlock

Madam,

With what language shall I address my lovely fair to acquaint her with the sentiments of a heart she delights to torture? I have not a minute's quiet out of your sight; and when I am with you, you use me with so much distance, that I am still in a state of absence, heightened with a view of the charms which I am denied to approach. In a word, you must give me either a fan, a mask or a glove you have worn, or I cannot live; otherwise you must expect that I'll kiss your hand, or, when I next sit by you, steal your handkerchief. You yourself are too great a bounty to be secured at once; therefore I must be prepared by degrees, lest the mighty gift distract me with joy.

Dear Miss Scurlock, I am tired with calling you by that name; therefore, say the day in which you will take that of, Madam, your most obedient, most devoted, humble servant,

Rich. Steele

August 1707 (two weeks before their wedding)

Madam,

It is the hardest thing in the world to be in love and yet attend to business. As for me all who speak to me find me out, and I must lock myself up or other people will do it for me.

A gentleman asked me this morning, 'What news from

Lisbon?' and I answered, 'She is exquisitely handsome.' Another desired to know when I had last been at Hampton Court. I replied, 'It will be on Tuesday come se'nniht.' Pr'ythee, allow me at least to kiss your hand before that day, that my mind may be in some composure. O love!

A thousand torments dwell about me!

Yet who would live to live without thee?

Methinks I could write a volume to you; but all the language on earth would fail in saying how much and with what disinterested passion I am ever yours—

Rich. Steele

7 October 1707

My Loved Creature,

I write this only to bid you good-night and assure you of my diligence in the matter I told you of.

You may assure yourself I value you according to your merit which is saying that you have my heart by all the ties of beauty, virtue, good nature and friendship. I find by the progress I have made to-night, that I shall do my business effectually in two days' time. Write me word you are in good humour which will be the highest pleasure to your obliged husband,

Rich. Steele

I shall want some linen from your house tomorrow.

George Farquhar
1676/7–1707

George Farquhar was born in Londonderry, the son of a clergyman, and educated at Trinity College, Dublin. On leaving Trinity, he tried his hand as an actor, but suffered from paralysing stage fright. He made his way to London where his first play, *Love and a Bottle*, was staged in 1698, telling the story of an Irishman newly arrived in the city who is a great success with the ladies. By all accounts, Farquhar was himself both handsome and charming, a wit and a troublemaker.

One night in a tavern, Farquhar heard a young woman named Anne Oldfield reading aloud behind the bar. He was so convinced by her talent that he introduced her to friends in the theatre, and she was taken on as an actress at Drury Lane.

George and Anne's liaison was not long lasting, and in 1703 George married a widow named Margaret Pemell. He had money troubles all his life, and health problems, but even when his difficulties were at their height he was still writing his dazzling and iconoclastic comedies, the best-known of which is probably *The Recruiting Officer*.

Anne Oldfield began a long-term relationship with an MP named Arthur Mainwaring at around the same time as George's marriage. Her career went from strength to strength, and by the time she died in 1730 she was both rich and famous. She is buried in Westminster Abbey.

To Anne Oldfield, Sunday, after Sermon (1699?)

I came, I saw, and was conquered; never had man more to say, yet can I say nothing; where others go to save their souls, there have I lost mine; but I hope that Divinity which has the justest title to its service has received it; but I will endeavour to suspend these raptures for a moment, and talk calmly–

Nothing on earth, madam, can charm, beyond your wit but your beauty: after this not to love you would proclaim me a fool; and to say I did when I thought otherwise would pronounce me a knave; if anybody called me either I should resent it; and if you but think me either I shall break my heart.

You have already, madam, seen enough of me to create a liking or an aversion; your sense is above your sex, then let your proceeding be so likewise, and tell me plainly what I have to hope for. Were I to consult my merits my humility would chide any shadow of hope; but after a sight of such a face whose whole composition is a smile of good nature, why should I be so unjust as to suspect you of cruelty. Let me either live in *London* and be happy or retire again to my desert to check my vanity that drew me thence; but let me beg you to receive my sentence from your own mouth, that I may hear you speak and see you look at the same time; then let me be unfortunate if I can.

If you are not the lady in mourning that sat upon my right hand at church, you may go to the devil, for I'm sure you're a witch.

Alexander Pope
1688–1744

The brilliant Alexander Pope was a poet, critic, essayist, satirist, garden designer, art connoisseur,
letter-writer and wit. He was dogged throughout his
life by ill health; this was attributed to his spending too
much time at his books, but in fact he had tuberculosis of the bone, contracted in infancy, which left him
small, crippled and plagued with various tiresome ail-
ments. He was a great feuder, but also had a large
circle of devoted friends. He loved female society and
was clearly extraordinarily charming, but while
women enjoyed his attentions and his wit, his deeper
feelings were never reciprocated.

Particular among his friends were two sisters,
Martha and Teresa Blount, and he corresponded with
both, writing at one point to Teresa, 'My violent
passion for your fair self and your sister has been
divided, and with the most wonderful regularity in the
world. Even from my infancy I have been in love with
one after the other of you week by week.' Pope never
married, and Martha was the chief beneficiary of his
will.

Four letters follow: one to each of the Blount

sisters, and two to Lady Mary Wortley Montagu, another intimate, married to a diplomat and living in Constantinople.

To Martha Blount, 1714

Most Divine,

It is some proof of my sincerity towards you, that I write when I am prepared by drinking to speak truth; and sure a letter after twelve at night must abound with that noble ingredient. That heart must have abundance of flames, which is at once warmed by wine and you: wine awakens and expresses the lurking passions of the mind, as varnish does the colours that are sunk in a picture, and brings them out in all their natural glowing. My good qualities have been so frozen and locked up in a dull constitution at all my former sober hours, that it is very astonishing to me, now I am drunk, to find so much virtue in me.

In these overflowings of my heart I pay you my thanks for these two obliging letters you favoured me with of the 18th and 24th instant. That which begins with 'My charming Mr Pope!' was a delight to me beyond all expression; you have at last entirely gained the conquest over your fair sister. It is true you are not handsome, for you are a woman, and think you are not: but this good humour and tenderness for me has a charm that cannot be resisted. That face must needs be irresistible which was adorned with smiles, even when it could not see the coronation! [of George I, in September 1714] I do suppose you will not show this epistle out of vanity, as I doubt not your sister does all I write to her . . .

To Teresa Blount, *1716*

Madam,

– I have so much esteem for you, and so much of the other thing, that, were I a handsome fellow, I should do you a vast deal of good: but as it is, all I am good for, is to write a civil letter, or to make a fine speech. The truth is, that considering how often and how openly I have declared love to you, I am astonished (and a little affronted) that you have not forbid my correspondence, and directly said, *See my face no more!*

It is not enough, madam, for your reputation, that you have your hands pure from the stain of such ink as might be shed to gratify a male correspondent. Alas! While your heart consents to encourage him in this lewd liberty of writing, you are not (indeed you are not) what you would so fain have me think you – a prude! I am vain enough to conclude that (like most young fellows) a fine lady's silence is consent, and so I write on –

But, in order to be as innocent as possible in this epistle, I will tell you news. You have asked me news a thousand times, at the first word you spoke to me; which some would interpret as if you expected nothing from my lips: and truly it is not a sign two lovers are together, when they can be so impertinent as to inquire what the world does. All I mean by this is, that either you or I cannot be in love with the other: I leave you to guess which of the two is that stupid and insensible creature, so blind to the other's excellence and charms.

To Lady Mary Wortley Montagu, June 1717

Madam,
— If to live in the memory of others have anything desirable in it, 'tis what you possess with regard to me in the highest sense of the words.

There is not a day in which your figure does not appear before me; your conversations return to my thoughts, and every scene, place or occasion where I have enjoyed them, are as livelily painted as an imagination equally warm and tender can be capable to represent them.

You tell me, the pleasure of being nearer the sun has a great effect upon your health and spirits. You have turned my affections so far eastward that I could almost be one of his worshippers: for I think the sun has more reason to be proud of raising your spirits, than of raising all the plants, and ripening all the minerals in the earth.

It is my opinion, a reasonable man might gladly travel three or four thousand leagues to see your nature, and your wit, in their full perfection. What may not we expect from a creature that went over the most perfect of this part of the world, and is every day improving by the sun in the other. If you do not now write and speak the finest things imaginable, you must be content to be involved in the same imputation with the rest of the East and be concluded to have abandoned yourself to extreme effeminacy, laziness and lewdness of life . . .

For God's sake, madam, send to me as often as you can; in the dependence that there is no man breathing more constantly, or more anxiously mindful of you. Tell me that you are well, tell me that your little son is well, tell me that your very dog (if you have one) is well. Defraud me of no one thing that pleases you, for whatever that is, it will please me better than anything else can do. I am always yours.

To Lady Mary Wortley Montagu, after her return to England, 1719

I might be dead or you in Yorkshire, for anything that I am the better for your being in town. I have been sick ever since I saw you last, and now have a swelled face, and very bad; nothing will do me so much good as the sight of dear Lady Mary; when you come this way let me see you, for indeed I love you.

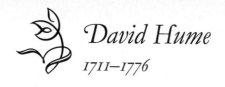

David Hume

1711–1776

David Hume was a philosopher, economist and historian; his great works include *A Treatise of Human Nature* and *An Enquiry Concerning Human Understanding*. He lived an exemplary scholarly life until 1763, when he visited Paris for the first time, and stayed for more than two years. He seems during this period to have suffered some kind of mid-life crisis; celebrated in the *salons* of the great Parisian ladies, he became particularly enamoured of one Madame de Boufflers, already the mistress of the prince de Conti. But the lady was a great deal more experienced than the philosopher in such flirtations, and the smitten Hume grew more and more confused. When her husband died, it became clear that she hoped to marry the prince, and Hume ultimately found himself in the rather unsatisfactory role of confidant to both.

To Madame de Boufflers, 3 April 1766

It is impossible for me, dear madam, to express the difficulty which I have to bear your absence, and the continual want which I feel of your society. I had accustomed myself, of a long time, to think of you as a friend from whom I was never to be separated during any considerable time; and I had flattered myself that we were fitted to pass our lives in intimacy and cordiality with each other. Age and a natural equality of temper were in danger of reducing my heart to too great indifference about everything, it was enlivened by the charms of your conversation, and the vivacity of your character. Your mind, more agitated both by unhappy circumstances in your situation and by your natural disposition, could repose itself in the more calm sympathy which you found with me.

But behold! three months are elapsed since I left you; and it is impossible for me to assign a time when I can hope to join you. I still return to my wish, that I had never left Paris, and that I had kept out of the reach of all other duties, except that which was so sweet, and agreeable, to fulfil, the cultivating your friendship and enjoying your society. Your obliging expressions revive this regret in the strongest degree; especially where you mention the wounds which, though skinned over, still fester at the bottom.

Oh! my dear friend, how I dread that it may still be long ere you reach a state of tranquillity, in a distress which so little admits of any remedy, and which the natural elevation of your character, instead of putting you above it, makes you feel with greater sensibility. I could only wish to administer the temporary consolation, which the presence of a friend never fails to afford . . . I kiss your hands with all the devotion possible.

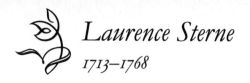

Laurence Sterne
1713–1768

Laurence Sterne's masterpiece was *Tristram Shandy*, or, more properly, *The Life and Opinions of Tristram Shandy, Gentleman*, published in nine volumes between 1759 and 1767. It was an immediate success, and Sterne was fêted both at home and in Europe. The risqué wit and satire of *Tristram Shandy* shocked some readers, and seemed to them to be at odds with the author's profession; Sterne was a clergyman, and published several volumes of sermons. His paradoxical nature – the licentious moralist and sceptical Christian – is illustrated by the second letter here, to Lady Percy, in which he is trying hard to engineer a clandestine meeting while pretending to leave it all in the lap of the gods.

Sterne's marriage was widely known to be unhappy; his wife Elizabeth Lumley was described by her own cousin as 'a Woman of great integrity & many virtues, but they stand like quills upon the fretfull porcupine'. He had many love affairs, the most enduring with Catherine Fourmantel, a celebrated singer.

To Catherine Fourmantel, 8 May 1760

My dear Kitty,

– I have arrived here safe and sound except for the hole in my heart, which you have made, like a dear, enchanting slut as you are. And now my dear, dear girl! let me assure you of the truest friendship for you, that ever man bore towards a woman. Where ever I am, my heart is warm towards you and ever shall be till it is cold for ever.

I thank you for the kind proof you gave me of your love and of your desire to make my heart easy, in ordering yourself to be denied to you know who: – whilst I ham [sic] so miserable to be separated from my dear dear Kitty, it would have stabbed my soul to have thought such a fellow could have the liberty of comeing near you. I therefore take this proof of your love and good principles most kindly, and have as much faith and dependence upon you in it as if I were at your elbow – would to God I was at it this moment! but I am sitting solitary and alone in my bedchamber (ten o'clock at night after the play) and would give a guinea for a squeeze of your hand. I send my soul perpetually out to see what you are a-doing – wish I could send my body with it.

Adieu! dear and kind girl, and believe me ever your kind friend and most affectionate admirer. I go to the Oratorio this night. Adieu! Adieu!

P.S. –My service to your Mama.

Direct to me in the Pall Mal at ye 2nd House from St Alban's Street

To Lady Percy
Sent from the Mount Coffee House, Tuesday, 3 o'clock

There is a strange mechanical effect produced in writing a billet-doux within a stone cast of the lady who engrosses the heart and soul of an *inamoratos*. For this cause (but mostly because I am to dine in this neighbourhood) have I, Tristram Shandy, come forth from my lodgings to a coffee-house, the nearest I could find to my dear Lady's house, and have called for a sheet of gilt paper to try the truth of this article of my creed – now for it –

O my dear Lady, what a dishclout of a soul has thou made of me! – I think, by the by, this a little too familiar an introduction for so unfamiliar a situation as I stand in with you – where, heaven knows, I am kept at a distance and despair of getting an inch nearer you, with all the steps and windings I can think of to recommend myself to you. Would not any man in his senses run diametrically from you, and as far as his legs would carry him, rather than thus causelessly, foolishly and foolhardily, expose himself afresh and afresh, where his heart and his reason tell him he shall be sure to come off loser, if not totally undone.

Why would you tell me you would be glad to see me? Does it give you pleasure to make me more unhappy, or does it add to your triumph, that your eyes and lips have turned a man into a fool, whom the rest of the town is courting as a wit?

I am a fool, the weakest, the most ductile, the most

tender fool that ever woman tried the weakness of, and the most unsettled in my purposes and resolutions of recovering my right mind.

It is but an hour ago that I kneeled down and swore I never would come near you, and after saying my Lord's Prayer for the sake of the close, *of not being led into temptation*, out I sallied like any Christian hero, ready to take the field against the world, the flesh and the devil; not doubting but I should finally trample them all down under my feet.

And now I am got so near you, within this vile stone's cast of your house, I feel myself drawn into a vortex, that has turned my brain upside downwards; and though I had purchased a box ticket to carry me to Miss —'s benefit, yet I knew very well that was a single line directed to me to let me know Lady — would be alone at seven, and suffer me to spend the evening with her, she would infallibly see everything verified as I have told her.

I dine at Mr C—r's in Wigmore Street, in this neighbourhood, where I shall stay till seven, in hopes you purpose to put me to this proof. If I hear nothing by that time, I shall conclude you are better disposed of, and shall take a sorry hack and sorrily jog on to the play. Curse on the word, I know nothing but sorrow, except the one thing that I love you (perhaps foolishly, but) most sincerely,

L. Sterne

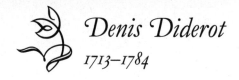

Denis Diderot
1713–1784

Denis Diderot, philosopher, novelist and polymath, was born in the eastern French city of Langres. After gaining his degree, he abandoned his original plan to study for the priesthood, and instead started studying law; he abandoned this in turn in 1734, and declared his intention to become a writer, thus alienating his family. They were further alienated by his marriage to Antoinette Champion, a devout Roman Catholic, whom they regarded as socially inferior, poorly educated and too old (she was four years his senior). In the event, the marriage was not happy, and in 1755 Diderot began a love affair with Sophie Volland, which lasted until her death.

As is the case with many Great Men, Diderot was always short of money. He spent almost twenty-five years compiling one of the first encyclopaedias, a project which the French authorities saw as dangerously seditious, and Diderot was constantly harassed as he worked on it. In the end, Catherine the Great of Russia, hearing of his money troubles, offered to buy his library; she then told him it was to be kept in Paris, and she would pay him as its custodian. After his death, the library was shipped to St Petersburg, where today it remains in the collection of the National Library of Russia.

To Sophie Volland, July 1759

I cannot leave this place without saying a few words to you. So, my pet, you expect a good deal from me. Your happiness, your life, even, depend, you say, upon my ever loving you!

Never fear, my dear Sophie; that will endure, and you shall live, and be happy. I have never committed a crime yet, and am not going to begin. I am wholly yours – you are everything to me; we will sustain each other in all the ills of life it may please fate to inflict upon us; you will soothe my troubles; I will comfort you in yours. Would that I could always see you as you have been lately! As for myself, you must confess that I am just as I was on the first day you saw me.

This is no merit of my own; but I owe it in justice to myself to tell you so. It is one effect of good qualities to be felt more vividly from day to day. Be assured of my constancy to yours, and of my appreciation of them. Never was a passion more justified by reason than mine. Is it not true, my dear Sophie, that you are very amiable? Examine yourself – see how worthy you are of being loved; and know that I love you very much. That is the unvarying standard of my feelings.

Good night, my dear Sophie. I am as happy as man can be in knowing that I am loved by the best of women.

To Sophie Volland, Au Grandval, 20 October 1759

You are well! You think of me! You love me. You will always love me. I believe you: now I am happy. I live again. I can talk, work, play, walk – do anything you wish. I must have made myself very disagreeable the last two or three days. No! my love; your very presence would not have delighted me more than your first letter did.

How impatiently I waited for it! I am sure my hands trembled when opening it. My countenance changed; my voice altered; and unless he were a fool, he who handed it to me would have said – 'That man receives news from his father or mother, or someone else he loves.' I was just at that moment about to send you a letter expressing my great uneasiness. While you are amusing yourself, you forget how much my heart suffers . . .

Adieu, my dearest love. My affection for you is ardent and sincere. I would love you even more than I do, if I knew how.

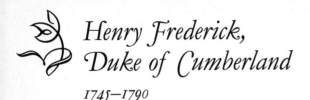

Henry Frederick, Duke of Cumberland
1745–1790

Henry Frederick was the brother of George III. His affair with the married Henrietta Vernon, Lady Grosvenor, caused a great scandal; the lovers were not discreet, and the Duke pursued Lady Grosvenor up and down the country disguised as first 'a Welshman' (whatever that entailed) and then 'a farmer'. Lord Grosvenor brought an action for 'criminal conversation' (adultery) against him, and the jury, having been shown some of the lovers' correspondence, awarded damages against the Duke of £10,000. The letters were stolen, published and caused a sensation all over London. As this one demonstrates, the Duke's ardour was great, if somewhat inarticulate.

To Lady Grosvenor

My dear little Angel,
— I wrote my last letter to you yesterday at eleven o'clock just when we sailed I dined at two o'clock and as for the afternoon I had some music I have my own servant a-board that plays

... and so got to bed about 10 – I then prayed for you *my dearest love kissed your dearest little hair* and laye down and dreamt of you had you on the dear little *couch* ten thousand times in my arms kissing you and telling you how much I loved and adored you and you seem pleased but alas when I woke it found it all dillusion *nobody by me but myself at sea* ... I am sure the account of this days duty can be no pleasure to you my love yet it is exactly what I have done and as I promised you always to let you know my motions and thoughts I have now performed my promise this day to you and always will until the very last letter you shall have from me.

When I shall return to you that instant O' my love mad and happy beyond myself to tell you how I love you and have thought of you ever since I have been separated from you ... I hope you are well I am sure I need not tell you I have had nothing in my thoughts but your dearself and long for the time to come back again to you I will all the while take care of myself because you desire *my dear little Friend* does the angel of my heart pray do you take care of your dearself for the sake of your faithful servant who lives but to love you to adore you, and to bless the moment that has made you generous enough to own it to him I hope my dear nay I will dare to say you never will have reason to repent it ...

Indeed my dear angel I need not tell you I know you read the reason too well that made me do so it was to write to you for God knows I wrote to no one else nor shall I at any other but to the King God bless you most amiable and dearest little creature living ...

God bless you till I shall again have an opportunity of sending to you, I shall write to you a letter a day as many days as you miss herein of me when I do they shall all come Friday 16th June God bless I shant forget you God knows you have told me so before I have your heart and it lies warm at my breast I hope mine feels as easy to you thou joy of my life adieu.

Wolfgang Amadeus Mozart
1756–1791

Wolfgang Amadeus Mozart was one of the most talented, prolific and influential composers the world has ever seen. He was born in Salzburg, and was playing and composing from the age of five. He spent a great deal of his childhood touring the courts of Europe with his family, astounding audiences with his precocity.

The opportunities in Salzburg for a musician and composer of his breadth and brilliance were limited, and it was on a later trip around Europe, at Mannheim in Germany, that Mozart met and fell in love with Aloysia Weber, a singer. They were parted when he returned home, and when they met again two years later, Aloysia was no longer interested in him, and according to some accounts failed even to recognize him.

A few years later, in Vienna, Mozart encountered the Weber family again. Aloysia had married an actor, and Mozart turned his attention to her younger sister, Constanze, whom he married in 1782; they had six children, only two of whom survived infancy.

The Mozarts' fortunes fell and rose according to fashion and whether or not Mozart felt like writing the music that would please his potential patrons. They were undoubtedly extravagant, and inevitably posterity has sought to blame Constanze for their perennial problems with money. The letters between them suggest though that their marriage was a happy one, and they seem to have shared a childlike sense of humour (Mozart's jokes were almost obsessively scatological). Constanze accompanied Mozart on many of his numerous trips abroad, and after his tragic early death worked hard to preserve his legacy and enhance his reputation.

To Constanze, sent from Dresden, 16 April 1789

Dear little wife, I have a number of requests to make. I beg you
(1) not to be melancholy,
(2) to take care of your health and to beware of the spring breezes,
(3) not to go out walking alone – and preferably not to go out walking at all,
(4) to feel absolutely assured of my love. Up to the present I have not written a single letter to you without placing your dear portrait before me.
(6)* and lastly I beg you to send me more details in your

*Paragraphs 5 and 6 reversed in copy of letter in Berlin Library

letters. I should very much like to know whether our brother-in-law Hofer came to see us the day after my departure? Whether he comes very often, as he promised me he would? Whether the Langes come sometimes? Whether progress is being made with the portrait? What sort of life you are leading? All these things are naturally of great interest to me.

(5) I beg in your conduct not only to be careful of your honour and mine, but also to consider appearances. Do not be angry with me for asking this. You ought to love me even more for thus valuing our honour.

W. A. Mozart

To Constanze, sent from Vienna, 6 June 1791

I have this moment received your dear letter and am delighted to hear that you are well and in good spirits. Madame Leutgeb has laundered my nightcap and neck-tie, but I should like you to see them! Good God! I kept on telling her, '*Do let me show you how she (my wife) does them!*' – But it was no use. I am delighted that you have a good appetite – but whoever gorges a lot, must also shit a lot – no, walk a lot, I mean. But I should not like you to take *long walks* without me. I entreat you to follow my advice exactly, for it comes from my heart. Adieu – my love – my only one. Do catch them in the air – those 2999½ little kisses from me which are flying about, waiting for someone to snap them up. Listen, I want to whisper something in your ear – and you in mine – and now we open and close our mouths – again – again and again – at last we say: 'It is all about Plumpi – Strumpi – ' Well, you can think what you like – that is just why it's so convenient. Adieu. A thousand tender kisses. Ever your

Mozart

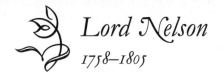

Lord Nelson
1758–1805

The legendary love affair between Lord Nelson and the great beauty Emma Hamilton began in Naples in 1798, where Emma was living with her husband, Sir William Hamilton, a diplomat more than thirty years her senior. Until her marriage, Emma had scraped by with jobs as an actress and artists' model and a murky career in London's *demi-monde*; she had been passed like a parcel to Sir William by his nephew, who had grown tired of her and who needed to marry an heiress, not a penniless courtesan. Sir William then confounded everyone by actually marrying Emma, for whom he seems to have had a genuine and deep regard.

Sir William also seems to have tolerated his wife's relationship with the naval hero quite happily, and the three of them lived as a *ménage-à-trois* after the Hamiltons' return to London in 1800. At the end of 1801, Emma gave birth to Nelson's daughter, Horatia.

Sir William died in 1803; Nelson in 1805 at the Battle of Trafalgar. His last letter to Emma, the second below, was found on his desk on HMS *Victory*; on it, Lady Hamilton has written, 'O miserable wretched Emma! O glorious and happy Nelson!'.

Despite Nelson's provisions for her in his will, and his pleas to his government to look after her should he be killed in battle, Emma was arrested and sent to debtor's prison in 1813. She escaped in 1814 and fled with Horatia to Calais, where she died in poverty the following year, probably of cirrhosis of the liver.

To Lady Hamilton

My Dearest Emma,
All your letters, *my dear letters*, are so entertaining, and which point so clearly what you are after that they give me either the greatest pleasure or pain. It is the next best thing to being with you.

I only desire, my dearest Emma, that you will always believe that Nelson's your own; Nelson's Alpha and Omega is Emma! I cannot alter – my affection and love is beyond even this world! Nothing will shake it but yourself; and that I will not allow myself to think for a moment is possible.

I feel that you are the real friend of my bosom, and dearer to me than life; and that I am the same to you. But I will neither have P's nor Q's come near you. No, not the slice of a single Gloster. But if I was to go on, it would argue that want of confidence which would be injurious to your honour.

I rejoice that you have had so pleasant a trip into Norfolk, and I hope one day to carry you there by a nearer *tie* in law, but not in love and affection than at present . . .

To Lady Hamilton
Victory, *19 October 1805, noon; Cadiz, SSE 16 leagues*

My dearest beloved Emma and the dear friends of my bosom, –The signal has been made that the enemy's combined fleet is coming out of port.

We have very little wind, so that I have no hopes of seeing them before to-morrow. May the God of Battles crown my endeavours with success! At all events I shall take care that my name shall ever be most dear to you and Horatia, both of whom I love as much as my own life; and as my last writing before the battle will be to you, so I hope in God that I shall live to finish my letter after the battle. May Heaven keep you, prays your Nelson and Bronte.

October 20th –In the morning we were close to the mouth of the straights, but the wind had not come far enough to the westward to allow the combined fleets to weather the shoals of Trafalgar, but they were counted as far as forty sail of ships-of-war which I suppose to be thirty-four of the line and six frigates. A group of them was seen off the lighthouse of Cadiz this morning, but it blows so very fresh, I think . . . that I rather believe they will go into harbour before night.

May God Almighty give us success over these fellows and enable us to get a Peace.

Robert Burns
1759–1796

Robert Burns was a poet of great repute when he met Mrs Agnes Maclehose at an Edinburgh tea party in 1787. Agnes ('Nancy') was married to James Maclehose, a Glasgow law agent, but had left him because of his cruelty and returned to Edinburgh. Almost at once she and Burns began a passionate correspondence and possibly a full-blown love affair. They used the pen-names 'Sylvander' and 'Clarinda' to protect their identities should their letters be discovered.

Burns was a hopeless (or, alternatively, terrific) womanizer, and rather impressively managed to impregnate Mrs Maclehose's maidservant Jenny Clow at the same time as carrying on the heated correspondence with her mistress. He was also maintaining a relationship with Jean Armour in Ayrshire, who had borne him twins in 1786 and was once again pregnant. In 1791, Mrs Maclehose and Robert Burns parted for the last time, and in 1792, she sailed for Jamaica, where her husband now lived, in order to try for a reconciliation. The attempt failed, and she returned to Edinburgh three months later, where she remained until her death in 1841.

To Mrs Agnes Maclehose, Tuesday evening, 15 January 1788

That you have faults, my Clarinda, I never doubted; but I knew not where they existed; and Saturday night made me more in the dark than ever. O, Clarinda! why would you wound my soul, by hinting that last night must have lessened my opinion of you. True, I was behind the scenes with you; but what did I see? A bosom glowing with honour and benevolence; a mind ennobled by genius, informed and refined by education and reflection, and exalted by native religion, genuine as in the climes of Heaven; a heart formed for all the glorious meltings of friendship, love, and pity. These I saw. I saw the noblest immortal soul creation ever showed me.

I looked long, my dear Clarinda, for your letter; and am vexed that you are complaining. I have not caught you so far wrong as in your idea – that the commerce you have with one friend hurts you, if you cannot tell every tittle of it to another. Why have so injurious a suspicion of a good God, Clarinda, as to think that Friendship and Love, on the sacred, inviolate principles of Truth, Honour and Religion, can be anything else than an object of His divine approbation? I have mentioned, in some of my former scrawls, Saturday evening next. Do allow me to wait on you that evening. Oh, my angel! how soon must we part! And when can we meet again! I look forward on the horrid interval with tearful eyes. What have not I lost by not knowing you sooner!

I fear, I fear, my acquaintance with you is too short to make that lasting impression on your heart I could wish.

Sylvander

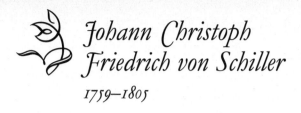

Johann Christoph Friedrich von Schiller

1759–1805

Schiller was a German poet, dramatist, historian and translator. He met Charlotte von Lengefeld in 1785, with her sister Karoline; after a correspondence of several years, Schiller married Charlotte in February 1790. This letter dates from August 1789, seven months before their wedding; evidently Schiller had asked Karoline to intercede for him with Charlotte, and had received an encouraging reply. Schiller and Charlotte had four children; he was troubled by ill-health for much of his life, and Charlotte outlived him by twenty years.

To Charlotte von Lengefeld, 3 August 1789

Is it true, dearest Lotte? May I hope that Karoline has read in your soul and has answered me out of your heart, what I did not have the courage to confess? Oh, how hard this secret has become for me, that I, as long as we have known each other, have had to conceal! Often, when we still lived together, I collected my whole courage and came to you with the intention to disclose it to you – but this courage always forsook me. I thought to discover selfishness in my wish, I feared that I had only my happiness in view, and that thought drove me back. Could I not become *to you* what you were to me, then my suffering would have distressed you, and I would have destroyed the most beautiful harmony of our friendship through my confession. I would have also lost that, what I had, your true and sisterly friendship. And yet again there come moments, when my hope arose afresh, wherein the happiness, which we could give each other, seemed to me exalted above every, every consideration, when I considered it even as noble to sacrifice everything else to it. You could be happy without me – but not become unhappy through me. This I felt alive in me – and thereupon I built my hopes.

You could give yourself to another, but none could love you more purely or more completely than I did. To none could your happiness be holier, as it was to me, and always will be. My whole existence, everything that lives within me, everything, my most precious, I devote to you, and if I try to ennoble myself, that is done, in order to become ever worthier of you, to make you ever happier. Nobility of souls is a beautiful and indestructible bond of friendship and of love. Our friendship and love become indestructible and eternal like the feelings upon which we establish them.

Now forget everything that could put constraint on your heart, and allow your feelings to speak alone. Confirm to me, what Karoline had allowed me hope. Tell me that you will be *mine* and that my happiness costs you no sacrifice.

Oh, assure me of that, it only needs a single word. Our hearts have a long time been close to each other. Allow the only foreign element which has hitherto been between us to vanish, and nothing, nothing to disturb the free communion of our souls. Farewell, dearest Lotte! I yearn for a quiet moment, to portray to you all the feeling of my heart, which, during that long period that this longing alone dwells in my heart, have made me happy and then again unhappy . . . Do not delay to banish my unrest for ever and always, I give all the pleasures of my life into your hand . . . Farewell, my most precious!

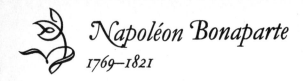

Napoléon Bonaparte
1769–1821

Napoléon, the humble soldier from Corsica who became a great general and Emperor of France, married Josephine de Beauharnais in March 1796. She was an impoverished Creole aristocrat from the French colony of Martinique with two children from an earlier marriage.

The first three letters here were written shortly after their wedding, when Napoléon had become commander of the French forces in Italy; the fourth dates from the Austrian war of 1805. In these letters, Napoléon casts himself as the supplicant, at the mercy of his beautiful and hard-hearted wife, who sometimes even insists on using the formal *vous* instead of the affectionate *tu*; there is something touching and almost comical about his anxious pursuit of Josephine all over Italy while conducting the military campaign that would make his name. It became clear to both later on in their marriage that neither had remained faithful, and Josephine's extravagance was a constant source of friction between them, but it seems from these early letters that Napoléon was very much in love with his wife.

Napoléon divorced Josephine in 1810 to marry Archduchess Marie-Louise of Austria, in order to gain an heir and secure the succession. Josephine continued to live near Paris, and remained on good terms with her former husband until she died in 1814.

After his defeat by the British, Napoléon was exiled to the island of St Helena in 1815, where he died six years later.

To Josephine at Milan,
Sent from Verona, 13 November 1796

I do not love thee any more; on the contrary, I detest thee. Thou art horrid, very awkward, very stupid, a very Cinderella. Thou dost not write me at all, thou dost not love thy husband; thou knowest the pleasure that thy letters afford him, and thou dost not write him six lines of even haphazard scribble.

What do you do then all day, Madame? What matter of such importance is it that takes up your time from writing to your very good lover? What affection stifles and pushes on one side the love, the tender and constant love, which you have promised him? Who can be this marvellous, this new lover who absorbs all your instants, tyrannises your entire days, and prevents you from being solicitous about your husband? Josephine, beware, one fine night the doors will break open and I will be there.

In truth, I am anxious, my good *amie*, at not receiving your news; write me quickly four pages, and say those amiable things which fill my heart with sentiment and pleasure.

I hope before long to press you in my arms and shall shower on you a million burning kisses as under the Equator.

Bonaparte

To Josephine at Genoa
Sent from Milan, 27 November 1796, three o'clock afternoon

I arrive at Milan, I rush into your *appartement*, I have left everything to see you, to press you in my arms . . . you were not there; you run to towns where there are festivities; you leave me when I arrive, you do not care any more for your dear Napoléon. It was a caprice, your loving him; fickleness makes you indifferent to him. Accustomed to dangers, I know the remedy for the worries and ills of life. The misfortune that overtakes me is incalculable; I had the right to be spared this.

I shall be here till the 9th in the evening. Do not put yourself out; run after pleasures; happiness is made for you. The entire world is too glad to be able to please you, and only your husband is very, very unhappy.

Bonaparte

To Josephine, 1796

I have not spent a day without loving you; I have not spent a night without embracing you; I have not so much as drunk one cup of tea without cursing the pride and ambition which force me to remain apart from the moving spirit of my life. In the midst of my duties, whether I am at the head of my army or inspecting the camps, my beloved Josephine stands alone in my heart, occupies my mind, fills my thoughts. If I am moving away from you with the speed of the Rhône torrent, it is only that I may see you again more quickly. If I rise to work in the middle of the night, it is because this may hasten by a matter of days the arrival of my sweet love. Yet in your letter of the 23rd and 26th Ventôse, you call me *vous*. *Vous* yourself! Ah! wretch, how could you have written this letter? How cold it is! And then there are those four days between the 23rd and the 26th; what were you doing that you failed to write to your husband? . . . Ah, my love, that *vous*, those four days make me long for my former indifference. Woe to the person responsible! May he, as punishment and penalty, experience what my convictions and the evidence (which is in your friend's favour) would make me experience! Hell has no torments great enough! Nor do the Furies have serpents enough! *Vous!* *Vous!* Ah! how will things stand in two weeks? . . . My spirit is heavy; my heart is fettered and I am terrified by my fantasies . . . You love me less; but you will get over the loss. One day you will love me no longer; at least tell me; then I shall know how I have come to deserve this misfortune . . . Farwell, my wife: the torment, joy, hope and moving spirit of my life; whom I love, whom I fear, who fills me with tender feelings which draw me close to Nature, and with violent impulses as tumultuous as thunder. I ask of you neither eternal love, nor fidelity, but simply . . . *truth*, unlimited honesty. The day when you say 'I love you less', will mark the end of my love and the last day of my life. If my heart were base enough to love without being loved in return I would tear it to pieces. Josephine! Josephine! Remember what I have sometimes said to you: Nature has endowed me with a virile and decisive character. It has built yours out of lace and gossamer. Have you ceased to love me? Forgive me, love of my life, my soul is racked by conflicting forces.

My heart, obsessed by you, is full of fears which prostrate me with misery . . . I am distressed not to be calling you by name. I shall wait for you to write it.

Farwell! Ah! if you love me less you can never have loved me. In that case I shall truly be pitiable.

Bonaparte

P.S. —The war this year has changed beyond recognition. I have had meat, bread and fodder distributed; my armed cavalry will soon be on the march. My soldiers are showing inexpressible confidence in me; you alone are a source of chagrin to me; you alone are the joy and torment of my life. I send a kiss to your children, whom you do not mention. By God! If you did, your letters would be half as long again.

Then visitors at ten o'clock in the morning would not have the pleasure of seeing you. Woman!!!

To Josephine at Munich, 19 December 1805

Great Empress, not a letter from you since your departure from Strassburg. You have passed at Baden, at Stuttgart, at Munich, without writing us a word. That is not very admirable nor very tender! I am still at Brunn. The Russians are gone; I have a truce. In a few days I shall decide what I shall do. Deign from the height of your greatness, to occupy yourself a little of your slaves.

Napoléon

Daniel Webster
1782–1852

This letter, from Daniel Webster, American orator and statesman (and martyr to hay fever), might not strictly conform to what we think of as a love letter, but it is one of enormous affection and charm, written with such wit and grace to a young woman who had left her bonnet at his house after attending dinner there, that it seems worthy of inclusion.

To Josephine Seaton, 4 March 1844

My Dear Josephine,

I fear you got a wetting last evening, as it rained fast soon after you left our door; and I avail myself of the return of your bonnet, to express the wish that you are well this morning, and without cold.

I have demanded parlance with your Bonnet: have asked it how many tender looks it has noticed to be directed under it; what soft words it has heard, close to its side; in what instances an air of triumph has caused it to be tossed; and whether, ever, and when, it has quivered from trembling emotions, proceeding from below. But it has proved itself a faithful keeper of secrets, and would answer none of my questions. It only remained for me to attempt to surprise it into confession, by pronouncing sundry names, one after another. It seemed quite unmoved by most of these, but at the apparently unexpected mention of one, I thought its ribands decidedly fluttered!

I gave it my parting good wishes; hoping that it might never cover an aching head, and that the eyes which it protects from the rays of the sun, may know no tears but those of joy and affection.

Yours, dear Josephine, with affectionate regard.

Danl. Webster

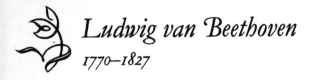

Ludwig van Beethoven
1770–1827

Ludwig van Beethoven revolutionized music and moved it on from the realm of aristocratic patronage – he was one of the first composers to rely on earnings rather than assorted rich benefactors for his living. His combative nature is shown by the dedication of his Third Symphony; originally it was to Napoléon, an almost exact contemporary and sometime hero, but then Napoléon declared himself Emperor, which so enraged Beethoven that he dedicated it instead to 'the *memory* of a great man'.

Beethoven's life was blighted by his increasing deafness – an unimaginably terrible affliction for a composer of his genius, and one which led him to the brink of suicide. He was by all accounts difficult, tortured, depressed and irascible – hardly surprising in the circumstances. He never married, although did fall deeply in love more than once, usually with one of his aristocratic and unattainable pupils.

Three passionate unsent love letters were found among Beethoven's papers after his death, addressed to his 'Immortal Beloved'. There was no year on the letters, and the identity of the 'Immortal Beloved' has not been conclusively established, although the most likely candidate is thought to be Antonie Brentano (1780–1869), a Viennese woman married to a Frankfurt merchant.

To 'Immortal Beloved', 6 July, morning

My angel, my all, my own self – only a few words to-day, and that too with pencil (with yours) – only till to-morrow is my lodging definitely fixed. What abominable waste of time in such things – why this deep grief, where necessity speaks? Can our love persist otherwise than through sacrifices, than by not demanding everything? Canst thou change it, that thou are not entirely mine, I not entirely thine? Oh, God, look into beautiful Nature and compose your mind to the inevitable. Love demands everything and is quite right, so it is *for me with you*, for *you with me* – only you forget so easily, that I must live *for you and for me* – were we quite united, you would notice this painful feeling as little as I should . . .

. . . We shall probably soon meet, even to-day I cannot communicate my remarks to you, which during these days I made about my life – were our hearts close together, I should probably not make any such remarks. My bosom is full, to tell you much – there are moments when I find that speech is nothing at all. Brighten up – remain my true and only treasure, my all, as I to you. The rest the gods must send, what must be for us and shall.

Your faithful
Ludwig

Monday evening, 6 July

You suffer, you, my dearest creature. Just now I perceive that letters must be posted first thing early. Mondays – Thursdays – the only days, when the post goes from here to K. You suffer – oh! Where I am, you are with me, with me and you, I shall arrange that I may live with you. What a life! So! Without you – pursued by the kindness of the people here and there, whom I mean – to desire to earn just as little as they earn – humility of man towards men – it pains me – and when I regard myself in connection with the Universe, what I am, and what he is – whom one calls the greatest – and yet – there lies herein again the godlike of man. I weep when I think you will probably only receive on Saturday the first news from me – as you too love – yet I love you stronger – but never hide yourself from me. Good night – as I am taking the waters, I must go to bed. Oh God – so near! so far! Is it not a real building of heaven, our Love – but as firm, too, as the citadel of heaven.

Good morning, on 7 July

Even in bed my ideas yearn towards you, my Immortal Beloved, here and there joyfully, then again sadly, awaiting from Fate, whether it will listen to us. I can only live, either altogether with you or not at all. Yes, I have determined to wander about for so long far away, until I can fly into your arms and call myself quite at home with you, can send my soul enveloped by yours into the realm of spirits – yes, I regret, it must be. You will get over it all the more as you know my faithfulness to you; never another one can own my heart, never – never! O God, why must one go away from what one loves so, and yet my life in W. as it is now is a miserable life. Your love made me the happiest and unhappiest at the same time. At my actual age I should need some continuity, sameness of life – can that exist under our circumstances? Angel, I just hear that the post goes out every day – and must close therefore, so that you get the L. at once. Be calm – love me – to-day – yesterday.

What longing in tears for you – You – my Life – my All – farewell. Oh, go on loving me – never doubt the faithfullest heart

Of your beloved

L

Ever thine.

Ever mine.

Ever ours.

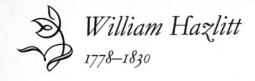

William Hazlitt
1778–1830

William Hazlitt was an essayist and critic who wrote on a variety of subjects from literature to prizefighting. His work was mocked by the same reactionary critics who tormented the poet John Keats; calling him 'Bill Hazlitt', they sneered at him as a failed artist and a 'manufacturer' of essays. His reputation undoubtedly suffered as a result of this, but also as a result of an unfortunate infatuation.

Hazlitt had married Sarah Stoddart, the daughter of a naval lieutenant, in 1808; by 1820, they had separated, and Hazlitt moved into rented rooms off Chancery Lane. It was here, on the morning of 16 August, that the twenty-year-old Sarah Walker, the landlady's daughter, brought him his breakfast. He fell instantly in love with her, and for the next three years rather lost his head. He decided he must have a divorce; remarriage after divorce was possible only under Scottish law, and so he set off for Scotland. While waiting in Edinburgh for the case to be completed, he rushed back intermittently to London, only to be consumed with jealousy at the idea that Sarah Walker was carrying on with another lodger called

John Tomkins. Sarah, to the puzzlement of Hazlitt (and presumably no one else), avoided him; he spent his time either trying to win her back or catch her out, at one point hiring an acquaintance to take a room in Chancery Lane to try to seduce her.

Hazlitt wrote a book about the whole experience, *Liber Amoris*, and although it was published anonymously, word of its authorship quickly got out. It was a gift to Hazlitt's enemies in the press – excruciatingly embarrassing and entirely lacking in dignity. And as a final humiliation, in 1824, Sarah had a son by Tomkins, with whom she lived until his death in 1858; she herself died twenty years later.

To Sarah Walker

– You will scold me for this, and ask me if this is keeping my promise to mind my work. One half of it was to think of Sarah; and besides I do not neglect my work either I assure you. I regularly do ten pages a day, which mounts up to thirty guineas' worth a week, so that you see I should grow rich at this rate, if I could keep on so; *and I could keep on so*, if I had you with me to encourage me with your sweet smiles, and share my lot. The Berwick smacks sail twice a week, and the wind sets fair. When I think of the thousand endearing caresses that have passed between us, I do not wonder at the strong attachment that draws me to you, but I am sorry for my own want of power to please. I hear the wind sigh through the lattice and keep repeating over and over to myself two lines of Lord Byron's tragedy –

So shalt thou find me ever at thy side,

Here and hereafter, if the last may be,

applying them to thee, my love, and thinking whether I shall ever see thee again. Perhaps not – for some years at least – till both thou and I are old – and then when all else have forsaken thee, I will creep to thee, and die in thine arms.

You once made me believe I was not hated by her I loved: and for that sensation – so delicious was it, though but a mockery and a dream – I owe you more than I can ever pay. I thought to have dried up my tears for ever the day I left you: but as I write this they stream again. If they did not, I think my heart would burst.

I walk out here on an afternoon and hear the notes of the thrush that comes up from a sheltered valley below, welcome in the spring; but they do not melt my heart as they used; it is grown cold and dead. As you say it will one day be colder. God forgive what I have written above; I did not intend it; but you were once my little all, and I cannot bear the thought of having lost your forever, I fear through my own fault. Has any one called? Do not send any letters that come. I should like you and your mother (if agreeable) to go and see Mr Kean in 'Othello' and Miss Stephens in 'Love in a Village', if you will, I will write to Mr T— to send you tickets. Has Mr P— called? I think I must send to him for the picture to kiss and talk to. Kiss me my best beloved. Ah! if you can never be mine, still let me be your proud and happy slave.

    H.

Lord Byron
1788–1824

'Byronic' has become shorthand for a particular type of romantic hero – pale, dark-haired, hollow-cheeked, cruel, reckless, irresistible to many women and therefore a source of deep irritation to the better behaved and more reliable sort of man so often and so inexplicably overlooked. Byron's behaviour, and his poetry, scandalized large parts of Europe to the extent that in 1924, a hundred years after his death, a petition for a memorial to him in Westminster Abbey was refused by the dean, whose opinion it was that 'Byron, partly by his openly dissolute life and partly by the influence of his licentious verse, earned a world-wide reputation for immorality among English-speaking people'.

Of the many entanglements of Byron's life, one of the most notorious was with the married Lady Caroline Lamb; in July 1813, it was rumoured that following a quarrel with him at a party, she tried to stab herself first with a knife, then with a broken glass. Eventually, she withdrew to Ireland, and the letter that follows was written to her there. The second letter was written to the Countess Guiccioli, a young woman married to a much older man, whom Byron met in

Venice in 1819; Byron inscribed his declaration on the flyleaf of a novel she had lent him.

To Lady Caroline Lamb

My dearest Caroline,
– If the tears, which you saw, and I know I am not apt to shed; if the agitation in which I parted from you – agitation which you must have perceived through the whole of this nervous affair, did not commence till the moment of leaving you approached; if all I have said and done, and am still but too ready to say and do, have not sufficiently proved what my feelings are, and must ever be, towards you, my love, I have no other proof to offer.

God knows I never knew till this moment the madness of my dear dearest and most beloved friend. I cannot express myself, this is no time for words – but I shall have a pride, a melancholy pleasure, in suffering what you yourself can scarcely conceive, for you do not know me.

I am about to go out with a heavy heart, for my appearing this evening will stop any absurd story to which the events of the day might give rise. Do you think now I am cold and stern and wilful? Will ever others think so? Will your mother ever? The mother to whom we must indeed sacrifice much more, much more on my part than she shall ever know, or can imagine.

'Promise not to love you'? Ah, Caroline, it is past promising! But I shall attribute all concessions to the proper motive, and never cease to feel all that you have already witnessed, and more than ever can be known, but to my own heart – perhaps, to yours. May God forgive, protect and bless you ever and ever, more than ever. –Your most attached

Byron

P.S. –These taunts have driven you to this, my dearest Caroline, and were it not for your mother, and the kindness of your connexions, is there anything in heaven or earth that would have made me so happy as to have made you mine long ago? And not less now than then, but more than ever *at this time.*

God knows I wish you happy, and when I quit you, or rather you, from a sense of duty to your husband and mother, quit me, you shall acknowledge the truth of what I again promise and vow, that no other, in word nor deed, shall ever hold the place in my affections which is and shall be sacred to you till I am nothing. You know I would with pleasure give up all here or beyond the grave for you, and in refraining from this must my motives be misunderstood?

I care not who knows this, what use is made of it – it is to you and to you only, yourself. I was, and am yours, freely and entirely, to obey, to honour, love and fly with you, *when*, *where*, and *how*, yourself might and may determine.

To the Countess Guiccioli, 25 August 1819

My dearest Teresa,

– I have read this book in your garden. My love, you were absent, or else I could not have read it. It is a favourite book of yours, and the writer was a favourite friend of mine. You will not understand these English words, and others will not understand them . . . which is the reason I have not scrawled them in Italian. But you will recognise the handwriting of him who passionately loved you, and you will divine that, over a book which was yours, he could only think of love.

In that word, beautiful in all languages, but most in yours – *amor mio* – is comprised my existence here and hereafter. I feel I exist here; and I feel I shall exist hereafter, to *what* purpose you will decide; my destiny rests with you, and you are a woman, seventeen years of age, and two out of a convent, I wish you had stayed there, with all my heart, or at least, that I had never met you in your married state. But all this is too late, I love you, and you love me – at least you *say* *so*, and *act*, as if you *did* so, which last is a great consolation at all events.

But I more than love you and cannot cease to love you. Think of me sometimes, when the Alps and ocean divide us, but they never will, unless you wish it.

Byron

John Keats
1795–1821

John Keats is now universally regarded as one of the greatest poets in the English language, but during his lifetime the powerful, aggressive and reactionary critics of the day – those same critics who had bullied William Hazlitt – treated him as an upstart (he had trained as an apothecary and his father was a stable-keeper, which apparently disqualified him from writing poetry), and mocked his work as vulgar and over-exuberant.

All his life, Keats was short of money and surrounded by illness and death – he lost his mother, his brother and an uncle to tuberculosis before he himself fell ill with it in 1820 at the age of twenty-four. His friend Charles Brown gives a heartbreaking account of Keats's first seeing a spot of blood on his sheet: 'I know the colour of that blood; – it is arterial blood; – I cannot be deceived in that colour; – that drop of blood is my death-warrant; – I must die.' He travelled to Italy in the hope of a cure, but died there a few months later. He was buried in Rome, and on his tombstone at his request was the inscription, 'Here lies one whose name was writ on water.'

The great love of Keats's life was a Hampstead neighbour, Fanny Brawne, to whom he was engaged. His passion for Fanny often shaded into jealousy, which in turn led to her posthumous reputation as a fickle and superficial flirt, although there seems to be little evidence for this. The facts suggest that she mourned Keats throughout the 1820s, befriending his sister as he had requested. She finally married a wealthy merchant named Louis Lindo in 1833.

To Fanny Brawne, 8 July 1819

My sweet Girl,
– Your letter gave me more delight than anything in the world but yourself could do; indeed, I am almost astonished that any absent one should have the luxurious power over my senses which I feel. Even when I am not thinking of you, I perceive your tenderness and a tenderer nature stealing upon me. All my thoughts, my unhappiest days and nights, have I find not at all cured me of my love of Beauty, but made it so intense that I am miserable that you are not with me: or rather breathe in that dull sort of patience that cannot be called Life. I never knew before, what such a love as you have made me feel, was; I did not believe in it; my Fancy was afraid of it, lest it should burn me up. But if you will fully love me, though there may be some fire, 'twill not

be more than we can bear when moistened and bedewed with Pleasures. You mention 'horrid people,' and ask me whether it depend upon them whether I see you again. Do understand me, my love, in this. I have so much of you in my heart that I must turn Mentor when I see a chance of harm befalling you. I would never see anything but Pleasure in your eyes, love on your lips, and Happiness in your steps. I would wish to see you among those amusements suitable to your inclinations and spirits; so that our loves might be a delight in the midst of Pleasures agreeable enough, rather than a resource from vexations and cares. But I doubt much, in case of the worst, whether I shall be philosopher enough to follow my own Lessons; if I saw my resolution give you a pain I could not. Why may I not speak of your Beauty, since without that I never could have lov'd you? I cannot conceive of any beginning of such love as I have for you but Beauty. There may be a sort of love for which, without the least sneer at it, I have the highest respect and can admire it in others; but it has not the richness, the bloom, the full form, the enchantment of love after my own heart. So let me speak of your Beauty, though to my own endangering; if you could be so cruel to me as to try else-where its Power. You say I am afraid I shall think you do not love me – in saying this you make me ache the more to be near you. I am at the diligent use of my faculties here, I do not pass a day without sprawling some blank verse or tagging some rhymes; and here I must confess that (since I am on that subject) I love you the more in that I believe you have liked me for my own sake and for nothing else. I have met with women whom I really think would like to be married to a Poem and to be given away by a Novel. I have seen your Comet, and only wish it was a sign that poor Rice would get well whose illness makes him rather a melancholy companion. And the more so as to conquer his feelings and hide them from me, with a forc'd Pun. I kissed your writing over in the hope you had indulged me by leaving a trace of honey. What was your dream? Tell it me and I will tell you the interpretation thereof.

    –Ever yours, my love! John Keats

To Fanny Brawne, 1820

Sweetest Fanny,
– You fear sometimes I do not love you so much as you wish? My dear Girl, I love you ever and ever and without reserve. The more I have known, the more have I lov'd. In every way, –even my jealousies have been agonies of Love; in the hottest fit I ever had I would have died for you. I have vexed you too much. But for Love! Can I help it? You are always new. The last of your kisses was ever the sweetest, the last smile the brightest; the last movement the gracefullest. When you pass'd my window home yesterday, I was fill'd with as much admiration as if I had seen you for the first time. You uttered a half complaint once that I only lov'd your beauty. Have I nothing else then to love in you

but that? Do I not see a heart naturally furnish'd with wings imprison itself with me? No ill prospect has been able to turn your thoughts a moment from me. This perhaps should be as much a subject of sorrow as joy – but I will not talk of that. Even if you did not love me I could not help an entire devotion to you: how much more deeply then must I feel for you knowing you love me. My Mind has been the most discontented and restless one that ever was put into a body too small for it. I never felt my Mind repose upon anything with complete and undistracted enjoyment – upon no person but you. When you are in the room my thoughts never fly out of window; you always concentrate my whole senses. The anxiety shown about our Loves in your last note is an immense pleasure to me; however, you must not suffer such speculations to molest you any more; nor will I any more believe you can have the least pique against me. Brown is gone out – but here is Mrs Wylie – when she is gone I shall be awake for you. Remembrances to your mother. – Your affectionate, J. Keats

To Fanny Brawne

My dearest Girl,
– I have been a walk this morning with a book in my hand, but as usual I have been occupied with nothing but you; I wish I could say in an agreeable manner. I am tormented day and night. They talk of my going to Italy. 'Tis certain I shall never recover if I am to be so long separate from you;

yet with all this devotion to you I cannot persuade myself into any confidence of you.

Past experience connected with the fact of my long separation from you gives me agonies which are scarcely to be talked of . . .

I am literally worn to death, which seems my only recourse. I cannot forget what has pass'd. What? Nothing with a man of the world, but to me deathful. I will get rid of this as much as possible. When you were in the habit of flirting with Brown you would have left off, could your own heart have felt one half of the one pang mine did. Brown is a good sort of Man – he did not know he was doing me to death by inches. I feel the effect of every one of those hours in my side now; and for that cause though, he has done me many services, though I know his love and friendship for me, though at this moment I should be without pence were it not for his assistance, I will never see or speak to him until we are both old men, if we are to be.

I *will* resent my heart having been made a football. You will call this madness. I have heard you say that it was not unpleasant to wait a few years, you have amusements – your mind is away – you have not brooded over one idea as I have, and how should you? You are to me an object intensely desirable – the air I breathe in a room empty of you is unhealthy. I am not the same to you – no – you can wait – you have a thousand activities – you can be happy without me. Any party, anything to fill up the day has been enough.

How have you passed this month? Who have you smil'd with? All this may seem savage in me. You do not feel as I do, you do not know what it is to love, one day you may, your time is not come. Ask yourself how many unhappy hours Keats has caused you in Loneliness. For myself I have been a Martyr the whole time, and for this reason I speak; the confession is forc'd from me by the torture. I appeal to you by the blood of that Christ you believe in: Do not write to me if you have done anything this month which it would have pained me to have seen. You may have altered – if you have not – if you still behave in dancing rooms and other societies as I have seen you – I do not want to live – if you have done so I wish this coming night may be my last.

I cannot live without you, and not only you but *chaste you*, *virtuous you*. The Sun rises and sets, the day passes, and you follow the bent of your inclination to a certain extent, you have no conception of the quantity of miserable feeling that passes through me in a day.

Be serious! Love is not a plaything – and again do not write unless you can do it with a crystal conscience. I would sooner die for want of you than – Yours for ever, J. Keats

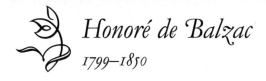

Honoré de Balzac
1799–1850

Honoré de Balzac was born in Tours. After studying law, he decided to devote his life to literature and, half-starving in a Parisian garret, he made ends meet by writing sensational novels on commission. He also became involved in several ill-advised commercial ventures in printing and publishing. In 1831, he began work on the great sequence of linked novels which became known as *La Comedie Humaine,* intended as a panoramic vision of French society; this was to occupy him for the next twenty years. Balzac's life was chaotic, his work habits eccentric, his health poor and his finances atrocious – he was unable to resist involving himself in various hare-brained money-making schemes – but *La Comedie Humaine* is regarded today as the first masterpiece of realism, and Balzac as one of the most influential writers in history.

In 1833, Balzac began a correspondence with the Countess Ewelina Hanska, who was married to a Polish landowner twenty years older than she. Their correspondence continued for seventeen years, and after the death of her husband in 1841 they travelled extensively together around Europe. They were eventually married on 15 March 1850; on 19 August of the same year, Balzac died.

To the Countess Ewelina Hanska

Oh! how I should have liked to remain half a day kneeling at your feet with my head on your lap, dreaming beautiful dreams, telling you my thoughts with languor, with rapture, sometimes not speaking at all, but pressing my lips to your gown! . . . O, my well-beloved Eva, the day of my days, the light of my nights, my hope, my adored one, my entirely beloved one, my only darling, when can I see you? Is it an illusion? Have I seen you? Ye gods! how I love your accent, just a shade thick, your mouth of kindness, of voluptuousness — allow me to say it of you, my angel of love. I am working night and day in order to go and see you for a fortnight in December. I shall pass over the Jura covered with snow; but I shall be thinking of the snowy shoulders of my love, my well-beloved. Ah! to breathe in your hair, to hold your hand, to clasp you in my arms — it is from these I get my courage! Some of my friends here are stupefied at the savage will-power I am displaying at this moment. Ah! they do not know my darling, she whose mere image robs grief of its stings. One kiss, my angel of the earth, one kiss tasted slowly, and then good-night!

To the Countess Ewelina Hanska
Sent from Dresden, 21 October 1843

I leave to-morrow, my seat is reserved, and I am going to finish my letter, because I have to put it in the post myself; my head is like an empty pumpkin, and I am in a state which disquiets me more than I can say. If I am thus in Paris, I shall have to return. I have no feeling for anything, I have no desire to live, I have no longer got the slightest energy, I seem to have no will-power left . . . I have not smiled since I left you . . .

Adieu, dear star, a thousand times blessed! There will perhaps come a moment when I shall be able to express to you the thoughts which oppress me. To-day I can only say that I love you too much for my repose, because after this August and September, I feel that I can only live near to you, and that your absence is death . . .

Adieu! I am going to take my letter to the post. A thousand tendernesses to your child a thousand times blessed; my friendly greetings to Lirette, and to you everything that is in my heart, my soul, and my brain . . . If you knew what emotion seizes me when I throw one of these packets in the box.

My soul flies towards you with these papers; I say to them like a crazy man, a thousand things; like a crazy man I think that they go towards you to repeat them to you; it is impossible for me to understand how these papers impregnated by me will be, in eleven days, in your hands, and why I remain here . . .

Oh yes, dear star, far and near, count on me like on yourself; neither I nor my devotion will fail you any more than life will fail your body. One can believe, dear fraternal soul, what one says of life at my age; well, believe me that there is no other life for me than yours. My task is done. If misfortune were to happen to you, I would go and bury myself in an obscure corner and ignored by everybody, without seeing anybody in the world; *allez*, this is not an empty word. If happiness for a woman is to know herself unique in a heart, alone, filling it in an indispensable manner, sure to shine in the intelligence of a man as his light, sure to be his blood, to animate each heart-beat, to live in his thought as the substance itself of that thought, and having the certainty that it would be always and always so; *eh bien*, dear sovereign of my soul, you can call yourself happy, and happy *senza brama*, for so I shall be for you till death. One can feel satiety for human things, there is none for divine things, and this word alone can explain what you are for me.

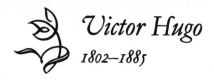

Victor Hugo
1802–1885

It is almost impossible to describe Victor Hugo without falling back on the word 'colossus'. He lived through most of a turbulent century in France, was exiled by Napoléon III for twenty years, and was, variously, a poet, a playwright, an essayist, a novelist, a painter and a politician. He was a monarchist who turned socialist, an aristocrat who became a champion of the poor.

Hugo was born of conflict. His father was an atheist republican and high-ranking officer in Napoléon's army; his mother a Catholic royalist. His parents were separated when he was small, and he lived for the most part with his mother. Adèle Foucher was a childhood friend with whom he fell in love, but his mother deemed the match unsuitable. It wasn't until after her death that he felt free to marry Adèle in 1822. Hugo was at that time primarily a poet, whose work received great acclaim. Hugo and Adèle had five children, but were not faithful to each other; in 1831, Adèle had an affair with the critic Saint-Beuve; in 1833, Hugo fell in love with Juliette Drouet, an actress, who for the next fifty years was his mistress, secretary and travelling companion; she died in 1882.

Victor Hugo's best-known works outside France are probably *Notre Dame de Paris* (1832) and *Les Misérables* (seventeen years in the writing, published in 1862). When he died, three million mourners followed his cortège to the Pantheon in Paris, where he was buried among France's greatest men.

To Adèle Foucher, January 1820

A few words from you, my beloved Adèle, have again changed the state of my mind. Yes, you can do anything with me, and tomorrow, I should be dead indeed if the gentle sound of your voice, the tender pressure of your adored lips, do not suffice to recall the life to my body. With what different feelings to yesterday's I shall lay myself down tonight! Yesterday, Adèle, I no longer believed in your love; the hour of death would have been welcome to me.

And yet I still said to myself, 'if it be true that she does not love me, if nothing in me could deserve the blessing of her love, without which there is no longer any charm in life, is that a reason for dying? Do I exist for my own personal happiness? No; my whole existence is devoted to her, even in spite of her. And by what right should I have dared to aspire to her love? Am I, then, more than an angel or a deity? I love her, true, even I; I am ready to sacrifice everything gladly for her sake – everything, even the hope of being loved by her; there is no devotedness of which I am not capable for her, for one of her smiles, for one of her looks. But could I be otherwise? Is she not the sole aim of my life? That she may show indifference to me, even hate, will be my misfortune, that is all. What does it matter, so that it does not injure her happiness? Yes, if she cannot love me I ought to blame myself only. My duty is to keep close to her steps, to surround her existence with mine, to serve her as a barrier against all dangers, to offer her my head as a stepping-stone, to place myself unceasingly between her and all sorrows, without claiming any reward, without expecting any recompense. Only too happy if she deign sometimes to cast a pitying look upon her slave, and to remember him in the hour of danger! Alas! if she only allow me to give my life to anticipate her every desire, all her caprices; if she but permit me to kiss with respect her adored footprints; if she but consent to lean upon me at times amidst the difficulties of life: Then I shall have obtained the only happiness to which I have the presumption to aspire. Because I am ready to sacrifice all for her, does she owe me any gratitude? Is it her fault that I love her? Must she, on that account, believe herself constrained to love me? No! she may sport with my devotion, repay my services with hate, and repulse my idolatory with scorn, without my having for a moment the right to complain of that angel; nor ought I to cease for an instant to lavish upon her all that which she would disdain. And should every one of my days have been marked by some sacrifice for her, I should still, at the day of my death, have discharged nothing of the infinite debt that my existence owes to hers.'

Such, my well-beloved Adèle, were the thoughts and resolutions of my mind at this time yesterday. Today they are still the same. Only there is mingled with them the certainty of happiness – such great happiness that I cannot think of it without trembling, and scarcely dare to believe in it.

Then it is true that you love me, Adèle? Tell me, can I trust in this enchanting idea? Don't you think that I shall end by becoming insane with joy if ever I can pass the whole of my life at your feet, sure of making you as happy as I shall be myself, sure of being adored by you as you are adored by me? Oh! your letter has restored peace to me, your words this evening have filled me with happiness. A thousand thanks, Adèle, my well-beloved angel. Would that I could prostrate myself before you as before a divinity. How happy you make me! Adieu, adieu, I shall pass a very happy night, dreaming of you.

Sleep well, and allow your husband to take the twelve kisses which you promised him, besides all those yet unpromised.

Nathaniel Hawthorne
1804–1864

Nathaniel Hawthorne was born in Salem, Massachusetts. A forebear, John Hathorne, was one of the judges who oversaw the Salem witch trials; Hawthorne might have added the 'w' to his surname to rid himself of this association. He was educated at Bowdoin College, and in 1837 went to work at the Boston Custom House. In 1842, he married Sophia Peabody, a painter, illustrator and member of the American Transcendentalist movement, whose members included Bronson Alcott, the father of Louisa May Alcott, the author of *Little Women*. After their marriage, the Hawthornes settled in Concord, Massachusetts, at the Old Manse, where they seem to have been very happy. In 1850, Hawthorne published his most famous novel, *The Scarlet Letter*, an immediate bestseller.

Four years after Nathaniel's death, Sophia moved to England; the family had lived there for four years between 1853 and 1857, when Nathaniel had been appointed United States Consul in Liverpool. She died in 1871, and was buried in Kensal Green Cemetery in London. In 2006, her remains were removed to the Hawthorne family plot in Concord, where she now lies next to her husband.

The most striking feature of this letter to Sophia, aside from the vast affection it conveys, is its immediacy; the voice is like that of a friend recounting a recent dream.

To Sophia

Unspeakably Belovedest,
— Thy letter has just been handed to me. It was most comfortable to me, because it gives such a picture of thy life with the children. I could see the whole family of my heart before my eyes, and could hear you all talking together . . .

The other night, I dreamt that I was at Newton, in a room with thee and with several people; and thou tookst occasion to announce that thou hadst now ceased to be my wife, and hadst taken another husband. Thou madest this intelligence known with such perfect composure and sang froid, — not particularly addressing me, but the company generally, — that it benumbed my thoughts and feelings, so that I had nothing to say. But, hereupon, some woman who was there present, informed the company that, in this state of affairs, having ceased to be thy husband, I had become hers, and, turning to me, very coolly inquired whether she or I should write to inform my mother of the new arrangement! How the children were to be divided, I know not.

I only know that my heart suddenly broke loose, and I began to expostulate with thee in an infinite agony, in the midst of which I awoke. But the sense of unspeakable injury and outrage hung about me for a long time, and even yet it has not quite departed. Thou shouldst not behave so when thou comest to me in dreams.

Oh, Phoebe, I want thee much. Thou art the only person in the world that ever was necessary to me. Other people have occasionally been more or less agreeable; but I think I was always more at ease alone than in anybody's company, till I knew thee. And now I am only myself when thou art within my reach. Thou art an unspeakably beloved woman. How couldst thou inflict such frozen agony upon me in that dream?

If I write any more, it would only be to express more lovings and longings; and as they are impossible to express, I may as well close.

Thy Husband

Benjamin Disraeli
1804–1881

Benjamin Disraeli, novelist and prime minister, grew up in London; his father was a literary man of independent means. The family converted from Judaism to Christianity in 1817. Disraeli initially studied as a lawyer, but gave it up to become a writer. He adopted a somewhat startling mode of dress (velvet trousers, patterned waistcoats, etc.), travelled around Europe and the Ottoman Empire, and wrote a number of novels with little success, one of which – a satire on London society – managed to offend several of his patrons. He also accrued huge debts.

In the 1830s, Disraeli turned to politics, and in 1837 became an MP. He also began courting Mary Anne Wyndham Lewis, the widow of one of his political sponsors. She was twelve years older than he, and her large income and London property were undoubtedly an attraction for Disraeli, but she was no fool, and as the letter below illustrates, she took some persuading as to the sincerity of his motives. She was eventually convinced, and they were married in August 1839.

Mary Anne – tiny, talkative, garishly dressed – was mocked as not quite the thing by smart society, but

she was an enormous help to Disraeli; she methodi-
cally and generously managed his horrific debts
('Dizzy' was of the 'pretend-it-isn't-happening-and-
pay-a-ruinous-rate-of-interest' school of financial
management), and was a talented political campaigner
and source of unstinting practical support. Once,
Disraeli, returning home late after a political triumph,
found her waiting up for him with a bottle of champagne and exclaimed, 'Why, my dear, you are more
like a mistress than a wife!', which, while not the most
tactful or romantic of compliments, should be seen in
the light of the fact that Mary Anne was seventy-five
at the time, and the two had been married for nearly
thirty years. Disraeli was heartbroken when she died
in 1872.

To Mary Anne Wyndham Lewis,
Sent from Park Street, Thursday night, 7 February 1839

I wd have endeavoured to have spoken to you of that which
it was necessary you shd know, & I wished to have spoken
with the calmness which was natural to one humiliated &
distressed. I succeeded so far as to be considered a 'selfish
bully' & to be desired to quit your house for ever. I have
recourse therefore to this miserable method of communicating with you; none can be more imperfect but I write as

if it were the night before my execution.

Every hour of my life I hear of an approaching union from all lips except your own. At last a friend anxious to distinguish me by some unusual mark of his favour & thinking to confer on me a distinction of which I shd be proud, offers me one of his seats for our happy month. The affair was then approaching absurdity. There was a period, & a much earlier one, when similar allusions to the future & intimations of what must occur were frequent from your lips; as if you thought some daily hint of the impending result was necessary to stimulate or to secure my affection.

As a woman of the world, which you are thoroughly, you ought not, you cannot be, unacquainted with the difference that subsists between our relative positions. The continuance of the present state of affairs cd only render you disreputable; me it wd render infamous. There is only one construction which Society, & justly, puts upon a connection between a woman who is supposed to be rich & a man whom she avowedly loves & does not marry. In England especially there is no stigma more damning; it is one which no subsequent conduct or position ever permits to be forgotten. It has crushed men who have committed with impunity even crimes; some things may indeed be more injurious; none more ignominious.

This reputation impends over me. I will at least preserve that honor which is the breath of my existence. At present I am in the position of an insolvent whose credit is not suspected; but ere a few weeks I must inevitably chuse between being ridiculous or being contemptible; I must be recognised as being jilted, or I must at once sink into what your friend Lady Morgan has already styled me 'Mrs Wyndham Lewis's De Novo'.

This leads me to the most delicat of subjects, but in justice to us both I will write with the utmost candor. I avow, when I first made my advances to you I was influenced by no romantic feelings. My father had long wished me to marry; my settling in life was the implied tho' not stipulated, condition of a disposition of his property, which wd have been convenient to me. I myself, about to commence a practical career, wished for the solace of a home, & shrunk from all the torturing passions of intrigue. I was not blind to worldly advantages in such an alliance, but I had already proved that my heart was not to be purchased. I found you in sorry, & that heart was touched. I found you, as I thought, aimiable, tender, & yet acute & gifted with no ordinary mind – one whom I cd look upon with pride as the partner of my life, who cd sympathise with all my projects & feelings, console me in the moments of depression, share my hour of triumph, & work with me for our honor and happiness.

Now for your fortune: I write the sheer truth. That fortune proved to be much less than I, or the world, imagined. It was in fact, as far as I was concerned, a fortune which cd not benefit me in the slightest degree; it was merely a jointure not greater than your station required; enough to maintain your establishment & gratify your private tastes. To eat & to sleep in that house & nominally to call it mine – these cd be only objects for a penniless adventurer. Was this an inducement for me to sacrifice my sweet liberty, & that indefinite future wh: is one of the charms of existence? No, when months ago I told you there was only one link between us, I felt that my heart was inextricably engaged to you, & but for that I wd have terminated our acquaintance. From that moment I devoted to you all the passion of my being. Alas! It has been poured upon the sand.

As time progressed I perceived in your character & mine own certain qualities, wh: convinced me that if I wished to persevere that profound & unpolluted affection wh: subsisted between us money must never be introduced. Had we married, not one shilling of your income shd ever have been seen by me; neither indirectly nor directly, wd I have interfered in the management of your affairs. If Society justly stigmatizes with infamy the hired lover, I shrink with equal disgust from being the paid husband.

You have branded me as selfish – Alas! I fear you have apparent cause. I confess it with the most heart rending humiliation. Little did I think when I wept, when in a manner so unexpected & so irresistible you poured upon my bosom the treasured savings of your affection, that I received the wages of my degradation! Weak, wretched fool! This led to my accepting your assistance in my trial; but that was stipulated to be a loan & I only waited for the bill which my agent gave me when you were at Bradenhaim as the balance of our accounts & which becomes due this very month, to repay it into yr bankers.

By heavens as far as worldly interests are concerned, your alliance cd not benefit me. All that society can offer is at my command; it is not the apparent possession of a jointure that ever elevates position. I can live, as I live, without disgrace, until the inevitable progress of events gives me that independence which is all I require. I have entered into these ungracious details because you reproached me with my interested views. No; I wd not condescend to be the minion of a princess; and not all the gold of Ophir shd ever lead me to the altar. Far different are the qualities which I require in the sweet participator of my existence. My nature demands that my life shall be perpetual love.

Upon your general conduct to me I make no comment. It is now useless. I will not upbraid you. I will only blame myself. All warned me: public and private − all were eager to save me from the perdition into which I have fallen. Coxcomb to suppose that you wd conduct yourself to me in a manner different to that in which you have behaved to fifty others!

And yet I thought I had touched your heart! Wretched Idiot!

As a woman of the world you must have foreseen this. And for the gratification of your vanity, for the amusement of ten months, for the diversion of your seclusion, could you find the heart to do this? Was there no ignoble prey at hand that you must degrade a bird of heaven? Why not have let your Captain Neil have been the minion of your gruesome hours with humiliating & debasing me. Nature never intended me for a toy & dupe. But you have struck deep. You have done that which my enemies have yet failed to do: you have broken my spirit. From the highest to the humblest scene of my life, from the brilliant world of fame to my own domestic hearth, you have poisoned all. I have no place of refuge: home is odious, the world oppressive.

Triumph – I seek not to conceal my state. It is not sorrow, it is not wretchedness; it is anguish, it is the *endurance* of that pang which is the passing characteristic of agony. All that can prostrate a man has fallen on my victim head. My heart outraged, my pride wounded, my honor nearly tainted. I know well that ere a few days can pass I shall be scoff & jest of that world, to gain whose admiration has been the effort of my life. I have only one source of solace – the consciousness of self-respect. Will that uphold me? A terrible problem that must quickly be solved.

Farewell. I will not affect to wish you happiness for it is not in your nature to obtain it. For a few years you may flutter in some frivolous circle. But the time will come when you will sigh for any heart that could be fond and despair of one that can be faithful. Then will be the penal hour of retribution; then you will recall to your memory the passionate heart that you have forfeited, and the genius you have betrayed.

D.

Charles Darwin
1809–1882

The single most important event of Charles Darwin's life came in 1831, when he was given the chance to travel to 'Terra del Fuego and home by the East Indies' aboard the *Beagle*, a surveying ship. The invitation was down to sheer luck – he certainly had no qualifications as a naturalist, having spent most of his time at university drinking, riding and gambling. The voyage changed him for ever. He left England an aimless young man, and returned five years later a scientist, whose observations would change the world.

By 1838, he decided it was time to be married – after drawing up a document in two columns, headed respectively 'marry' and 'not marry', like the great cataloguer he was. Under 'marry', he wrote, 'Constant companion . . . object to be beloved and played with . . . better than a dog anyhow . . . Only picture to yourself a nice soft wife on a sofa with good fire, & books & music'. The advantages elucidated in the 'not marry' column included 'conversation of clever men at clubs – not forced to visit relatives, & to bend in every trifle'. He became engaged to Emma

Wedgwood, a first cousin; the wedding took place in January 1839. They settled in London briefly – the letter here shows Darwin's excitement as he looked around the house where they were to live, presumably picturing 'a nice soft wife on a sofa' – and then moved to Down House in Kent, where they lived for the rest of their lives.

The marriage was a happy one, although the devout Emma feared for the effects of her husband's scientific discoveries on the fate of his immortal soul. Darwin's health was not good, and he worried about it constantly, as well as worrying about Emma's being upset by outraged criticism of his work; there is speculation that he delayed publishing his theory of evolution out of respect for her religiosity. They had ten children (three of whom died young), and despite his health concerns, Darwin lived to seventy-two. He is buried in Westminster Abbey, close to the monument to Isaac Newton. Emma died in 1896 and is buried in the churchyard at Downe.

To Emma Wedgwood
Sunday Night. Athenaeum. 20 January 1839

. . . I cannot tell you how much I enjoyed my Maer visit, – I felt in anticipation my future tranquil life: how I do hope you may be as happy as I know I shall be: but it frightens me, as often as I think of what a family you have been one of. I was thinking this morning how it came, that I, who am fond of talking and am scarcely ever out of spirits, should so entirely rest my notions of happiness on quietness, and a good deal of solitude: but I believe the explanation is very simple and I mention it because it will give you hopes, that I shall gradually grow less of a brute, it is that during the five years of my voyage (and indeed I may add these two last) which from the active manner in which they have been passed, may be said to be the commencement of my real life, the whole of my pleasure was derived from what passed in my mind, while admiring views by myself, travelling across the wild deserts or glorious forests or pacing the deck of the poor little 'Beagle' at night. Excuse this much egotism, –I give it you because I think you will humanize me, and soon teach me there is greater happiness than building theories and accumulating facts in silence and solitude. My own dearest Emma, I earnestly pray, you may never regret the great, and I will add very good, deed, you are to perform on the Tuesday: my own dear future wife, God bless you . . .

The Lyells called on me to-day after church; as Lyell was so full of geology he was obliged to disgorge, –and I dine there on Tuesday for an especial confidence. I was quite ashamed of myself to-day, for we talked for half an hour, unsophisticated geology, with poor Mrs Lyell sitting by, a monument of patience. I want practice in ill-treatment of the female sex, –I did not observe Lyell had any compunction; I hope to harden my conscience in time: few husbands seem to find it difficult to effect this. Since my return I have taken several looks, as you will readily believe, into the drawing-room; I suppose my taste [for] harmonious colours is already deteriorated, for I declare the room begins to look less ugly. I take so much pleasure in the house, I declare I am just like a great overgrown child with a new toy; but then, not like a real child, I long to have a co-partner and possessor.

Alfred de Musset
1810–1857

Alfred de Musset was born in Paris to a well-to-do literary family. A novelist, playwright and poet, he enjoyed great success before he was twenty.

In 1833, having read her second novel, Alfred de Musset wrote a letter to George Sand (the pseudonym of Amandine Aurore Lucile Dupin); they met, and he fell in love with her. She had left her husband, the Baron Casimir Dudevant, two years earlier. De Musset was twenty-three, and Sand twenty-nine.

George Sand had a burgeoning reputation as an editor and a novelist. Her cross-dressing and her male *nom-de-plume* had led people to make the predictable sneers about her sexuality and personal life, and her feminist and socialist principles meant that she constantly attracted criticism, but the number of people who fell in love with her suggests that she was a very charismatic woman.

In the letter here, Alfred de Musset declares himself for the first time, claiming that he has no hope of her returning his affection, and referring ruefully to a trip to Italy they had planned which he now assumes, in the light of his declaration, will have to be cancelled.

In fact, they became lovers and they did go to Italy together; the trip was an absolute disaster, and their relationship did not survive much longer.

De Musset died at the age of forty-seven; George Sand at the age of seventy-two, after an eventful life that contained many more adventures and love affairs.

To George Sand, 1833

My dear George,

— I have something stupid and ridiculous to tell you. I am foolishly writing you instead of having told you this, I do not know why, when returning from that walk. To-night I shall be annoyed at having done so. You will laugh in my face, will take me for a maker of phrases in all my relations with you hitherto. You will show me the door and you will think I am lying. I am in love with you. I have been thus since the first day I called on you. I thought I should cure myself in seeing you quite simply as a friend. There are many things in your character which could cure me; I have tried to convince myself of that as much as I could. But I pay too dearly for the moments I pass with you. I prefer to tell you and I have done well, because I shall suffer much less if I am cured by your showing me the door now. This night during which . . . [George Sand, who edited de Musset's letters for publication, crossed out the last two words, and with scissors cut out the following line] I had decided to let you know that I was out of town, but I do not want to make a mystery of it nor have the appearance of quarrelling without a reason. Now George, you will say: 'Another fellow, who is about to become a nuisance,' as you say. If I am not quite the firstcomer for you, tell me, as you would have told me yesterday in speaking of somebody else, what I ought to do. But I beg of you, if you intend to say that you doubt the truth of what I am writing, then I had rather you did not answer me at all. I know how you think of me, and I have nothing to hope for in telling you this. I can only foresee losing a friend and the only agreeable hours I have passed for a month. But I know that you are kind, that you have loved, and I put my trust in you, not as a mistress, but as a frank and loyal comrade. George, I am an idiot to deprive myself of the pleasure of seeing you the short time you have still to spend in Paris, before your departure for Italy, where we would have spent such beautiful nights together, if I had the strength. But the truth is that I suffer, and that my strength is wanting.

Alfred de Musset

Robert Schumann
1810–1856

Robert Schumann studied law at Leipzig and Heidelberg, but his real love was music. His piano teacher was Friedrich Wieck, whose daughter Clara, nine years younger than Robert, was already a talented pianist. Robert too was gifted, but an injury to his hand meant a career as a musician became impossible, and so he turned his attention to composition and criticism, founding an influential journal in which he championed new composers.

Robert and Clara fell in love when Clara was fifteen, and in 1837, Robert asked her father's permission for them to marry, which he withheld – Robert gives an account of the dreadful interview in the second letter below. For three years, the lovers battled for Friedrich's consent, going to court in the process; he never gave it, and so Robert and Clara were eventually married without it in 1840, the same year in which Robert composed many of his famous *Lieder*. Acclaim for Clara grew throughout Europe, and she showcased many of her husband's compositions, although he did not receive the same level of recognition as his wife.

Robert first experienced symptoms of mental illness in 1844, suffering from depression and delusions, but he had recovered by the following year. Ten years later, the symptoms returned, and he attempted suicide by throwing himself into the Rhine; he was rescued, but spent the remaining two years of his life in an asylum. Clara lived for another forty years.

To Clara Wieck, Leipzig, 1834

My dear and revered Clara,

– There are haters of beauty, who maintain that swans were really geese of a larger kind – one might say with equal justification that distance is only a close-up that has been pushed apart. And so indeed it is, for I speak with you daily (yes, even more softly than I usually do), and yet I know that you understand me. In the beginning I had various plans with regard to our correspondence. I wanted, for instance, to start a public one with you in the music journal; then I wanted to fill my air-balloon (you know that I own one) with ideas for letters, and arrange an ascent in a favourable wind with a suitable destination . . . I wanted to catch butterflies as letter-carriers to you. I wanted to send my letters first to Paris, so that you should open them with great curiosity, and then, more than surprised, would believe me in Paris. In short, I had many witty dreams in my head, from which only to-day the horn of the postilion [postman] has awakened me. Postilions, my dear Clara, have, by the way, as magical an effect on me as the most excellent champagne. One seems to have no head, one has such a delightfully light heart, when one hears them trumpeting so joyously out into the world. They are real waltzes of yearning to me, these trumpet-blasts, which remind us of something that we do not possess. As I said, the postilion blew me out of my old dreams into new ones . . .

To Clara, on her father's opposition to their marriage,
18 September 1837

— The interview with your father was terrible . . . Such frigidness, such disingenuousness, such deviousness, such contradictions — he has a new manner of destruction, he stabs you to the heart with the handle of the knife . . .

What now then, my dear Clara? I do not know what to do now — *not in the slightest.* My wits are going to pieces here, and in such a frame of mind one can assuredly not come to terms with your father. What now then, what now then? Above all, prepare yourself, and do *not once allow yourself to be sold* . . . I trust you, oh, *from all my heart,* and that is what upholds me . . . But you will have to be very *strong,* more than you dream of. Did not your father say those terrible words to me, that nothing can move *him;* he will *compel you by force,* if he fails in stratagem. Be afraid of everything!

I am to-day so dead, so *humiliated*, that I can hardly conceive a beautiful, good idea. So dishearted as to give you up I have not yet become; but so embittered, so hurt in my holiest feelings, so locked in a frame of the most ordinary commonplace.

If I only had a word from you! You must tell me what I am to do. Otherwise my being will turn to scorn and a byword, and I shall be off and away.

Not even to be allowed to see you! We could do so, he said, but in a neutral spot, in the presence of all, a regular show for everybody. How chilling all that is – how it rankles! We might even correspond, when you are on a journey! – that was all that he would consent to . . .

Give me consolation, dear God, that he may not let me perish in despair. I am torn up by the roots of my life.

Robert Browning
1812–1889

Elizabeth Barrett was a poet of some standing when Robert Browning, six years her junior, first wrote to her on 10 January 1845; it was a fan letter, but prefigured the many love letters that were to follow: 'I love your verses with all my heart, dear Miss Barrett.' Elizabeth was an invalid, and lived with her brothers and sisters and tyrannical father in Wimpole Street, London. Robert and Elizabeth met for the first time on 20 May 1845; shortly afterwards Robert rashly declared that he had fallen in love with her. Elizabeth, alarmed, withdrew somewhat; the two rebuilt their relationship on the basis of friendship. The turning-point came in the autumn of that year, when Elizabeth was advised to spend the winter in Italy for the sake of her health; her father refused to let her go, and Browning declared that he would marry her immediately to free her from her father's grasp. This time, Elizabeth was receptive, and they spent almost a year planning their escape, particularly the financial practicalities, as Elizabeth was sure that she would be disinherited by her father – which she was.

Robert and Elizabeth were married in secret at the

parish church of St Marylebone on 12 September 1846, and left immediately for Italy. Elizabeth gave birth to a son in 1849 at the age of forty-three. Her health was never good – there was no miraculous recovery, and she used opiates all her life – and there was no reconciliation with her father, despite her many efforts, but the couple were happy and productive; it was during her marriage that Elizabeth produced perhaps her greatest work, *Aurora Leigh*. They divided their time between Italy, France and London, until Elizabeth's death in Florence in 1861. Robert Browning lived another twenty-eight years, but never remarried, declaring that his heart was buried in Florence. He died in Italy; his body was returned to England, and he is buried in Poets' Corner in Westminster Abbey.

To Elizabeth Barrett:
Wednesday [postmarked 28 January 1846]

Ever dearest,
– I will say, as you desire, nothing on that subject – but this strictly for myself: you engaged me to consult my own good in the keeping or breaking our engagement; not *your* good as it might even seem to me; much less seem to another. My only good in this world – that against which all the world

goes for nothing – is to spend my life with you, and be yours. You know that when I *claim* anything, it is really yourself in me – you *give* me a right and bid me use it, and I, in fact, am most obeying you when I appear most exacting on my own account – so, in that feeling, I dare claim, once for all, and in all possible cases (except that dreadful one of your becoming worse again . . . in which case I wait till life ends with both of us), I claim your promise's fulfilment – say, at the summer's end: it cannot be for your good that this state of things should continue. We can go to Italy for a year or two and be happy as day and night are long. For me, I adore you. This is all unnecessary, I feel as I write: but you will think of the main fact as *ordained*, granted by God, will you not, dearest? – so, not to be put in doubt *ever again* – then, we can go quietly thinking of after matters. Till tomorrow, and ever after, God bless my heart's own, own Ba. All my soul follows you, love – encircles you – and I live in being yours.

To Elizabeth Barrett on the morning of their wedding day,
12 September 1846

You will only expect a few words. What will those be? When the heart is full it may run over; but the real fullness stays within . . . Words can never tell you . . . how perfectly dear you are to me – perfectly dear to my heart and soul. I look back and in every one point, every word and gesture, every letter, every *silence* – you have been entirely perfect to me –

I would not change one word, one look. My hope and aim are to preserve this love, not to fall from it – for which I trust to God, who procured it for me, and doubtless can preserve it. Enough now, my dearest own Ba! You have given me the highest, completest proof of love that ever one human being gave another. I am all gratitude – and all pride . . . that my life has been so crowned by you.

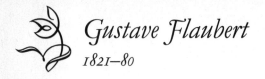

Gustave Flaubert
1821–80

The great novelist Gustave Flaubert is best known for *Madame Bovary*, his forensic examination of adultery, which led to his being prosecuted (unsuccessfully) for immorality. Arguably his most important female relationship was with his mother; Flaubert lived with her outside Rouen at Croisset on the Seine for much of his adult life. His one serious love affair was with Louise Colet, a prolific writer of poems, novels, essays and journalism, and a dazzling beauty who presided over a renowned Parisian *salon* and was confidante to many of the great writers of the age. He called her his 'Muse'; their relationship lasted from 1846–1854, but ended badly, and Colet later published a fictional account of it in her novel *Lui*. Flaubert also had a close relationship with George Sand.

Flaubert died at the age of fifty-nine of a stroke; his health had never been good, and he suffered from both syphilis and 'nervous fits', probably epilepsy. Louise Colet died in 1876.

To Louise Colet
Croisset, night of Saturday, 1 o'clock

You say to me very tender things, dear Muse. *Eh bien,* receive in exchange all those still more tender things than you could imagine. Your love ends by penetrating me like a lukewarm rain, and I feel myself soaked in it down to the very bottom of my heart. Hast thou not everything needful for me to love thee – body, mind, tenderness? You are simple of soul and strong of head, very little poetical, and extremely a poet; there is nothing but good in you, and you are entirely like your bosom, white and soft to the touch. Those I have known *va*, were not equal to you, and I doubt whether those that I have desired were your equal. I try sometimes to imagine to myself your face when you are old, and it seems to me that I shall love you as much, perhaps more.

To George Sand, 1866
Monday night

You are sad, poor friend and dear master; it was you of whom I thought on learning of Duveyrier's death. Since you loved him, I am sorry for you. That loss is added to others. How we keep these dead souls in our hearts. Each one of us carries within himself his necropolis.

I am entirely UNDONE since your departure; it seems to me as if I had not seen you for ten years. My one subject of conversation with my mother is you, everyone here loves you. Under what star were you born, pray, to unite in your person such diverse qualities, so numerous and so rare?

I don't know what sort of feeling I have for you, but I have a particular tenderness for you, and one I have never felt for anyone, up to now. We understood each other, didn't we, that was good.

I especially missed you last evening at ten o'clock. There was a fire at my wood-seller's. The sky was rose color and the Seine the color of gooseberry sirup. I worked at the engine for three hours and I came home as worn out as the Turk with the giraffe.

A newspaper in Rouen, the *Nouvelliste*, told of your visit to Rouen, so that Saturday after leaving you I met several bourgeois indignant at me for not exhibiting you. The best thing was said to me by a former sub-prefect: 'Ah! if we had known that she was here . . . we would have we would have . . . ' he hunted five minutes for the word; 'we would have smiled for her.' That would have been very little, would it not?

To 'love you more' is hard for me – but I embrace you tenderly. Your letter of this morning, so melancholy, reached the BOTTOM of my heart. We separated at the moment when many things were on the point of coming to our lips. All the doors between us two are not yet open. You inspire me with a great respect and I do not dare to question you.

Walter Bagehot
1826–1877

Walter Bagehot was a journalist, political commentator and economist, now most famous for his writings on the monarchy; he came from a prominent banking family in Somerset. Bagehot was very close to his mother, who was beautiful, affectionate and witty, but who had seen three of her five children die and was afflicted by psychotic episodes which cast a shadow over his childhood. He was encouraged in intellectual pursuits by his father, who had an extensive library.

A brilliant scholar, Bagehot took an MA from University College, London; he worked first as a lawyer, which he hated, and then as a banker, which he didn't really like any better, asserting that 'sums are a matter of opinion'. But his work at the bank in Bristol left him plenty of time for journalism. He founded a magazine, and from there graduated to editing the *Economist*, writing on a variety of political, economic and literary matters. In 1857, he became engaged to Eliza Wilson, the daughter of the *Economist*'s proprietor; they married in 1858 and settled in Somerset.

This charming letter, written during their engagement, attests to their initially passionate and happy relationship, but that state of affairs did not last. Bagehot was extraordinarily prolific, always up against a deadline, very sociable and fond of metropolitan life; Eliza could not share in his work or his enthusiasms, and grew increasingly withdrawn. They had no children.

To Elizabeth Wilson
Herd's Hill, 22 November 1857

My dearest Eliza,
I fear you will think the answer I wrote yesterday to your most kind and *delicious* letter, was very superficial, but I wrote it at once while people were talking and bothering me. I have now read yours over and over more times than I should like to admit. I awoke in the middle of the night and immediately lit a candle to read it a few times again. It has given me more pleasure than I ever received from a letter, and infinitely more than I thought it possible I could receive from one. I fancy that it is not now an effort to you to write to me – at least it reads as though it was written without effort. Yet it tells me things which with your deep and reserved nature it must have cost you much to put on paper. I wish indeed I could feel worthy of your affection – my reason, if not my imagination, is getting to believe you when you whisper to me that I have it, but as somebody says in Miss Austen, 'I do not at all mind having what is too good

for me'; my delight is at times intense. You must not suppose because I tell you of the wild, burning pain which I have felt, and at times, though I am and *ought* to be much soothed, still feel, that my love for you has ever been mere suffering. Even at the worst there was a wild, delicious excitement which I would not have lost for the world. At first, and before the feeling was very great it was simple pleasure to me to come to Claverton, and the charm of our early intellectual talks was very great, although of late, and particularly since the day in the conservatory, the feeling has been too eager not to have a good deal of pain in it, and the tension of mind has really been very great at times, still the time that I have known and loved you is immensely the happiest I have ever known. My spirits always make me cheerful in a superficial way, but they do not *satisfy*, and somehow life even before I was engaged to you was sweeter and gentler, and the jars and jangles of action lost their influence, and literature had a new value since *you* liked my writing, and everything has had a gloss upon it. Though I have come to Claverton the last few times with the notion that the gloss would go – that I should burst out and you would be tranquil and kind and considerate and *refuse* and I should never see you again. I had a vision of the thing which I keep by me. As it has *not* happened I am afraid this is egotistical – indeed I know it is – but I am not sure that egotism is bad in letters, and if I write to you I *must* write about what I feel for you. It is odd how completely our feelings change. No one can tell the effort it was to me to tell you I loved you – why I do not know, but it made me gasp for breath, and now it is absolutely pleasure to me to tell it to you and bore you with it in every form, and I should like to write it in big letters I LOVE YOU all across the page by way of emphasis. I know you will think me very childish and be shaken in your early notion that I am intellectual, but I cannot help it. This is my state of mind.

To change the subject, what is the particular advantage of being rubbed at *Edinburgh*? Since yesterday I have made careful enquiries and am assured that the English can rub. Why not be rubbed in Somersetshire? Let the doctor mark the place and have a patch put to show where and let any able-bodied party in the West of England rub on the *same* place and surely it will be as well? Does the man's touch do good to disease like the King's?

By incredible researches in an old box I have found the poem I mentioned to you. I wish I had not, for I thought it was better. I have not seen it for several years and it is not so good as I fancied – perhaps not good at all – but I think you may care to read it and you can't read it unless I send it and therefore I do send it. The young lady's name is Orithyia. The Greek legend is that she was carried away by the north wind. I have chosen to believe that she was in love with the north wind, but I am not aware that she ever declared her feelings explicitly in any document. By the way, you have. I have just read your letter in that light and I go about murmuring, 'I have made that dignified girl *commit* herself, I have, I have', and then I vault over the sofa with exultation. Those are the feelings of the person you have connected yourself with. *Please* don't be offended at my rubbish. Sauciness is my particular line. I am always rude to everybody I respect. I could write to you of the deep and serious feelings which I hope you believe really are in my heart, but my pen jests of itself and always will.

Yours with the fondest and deepest love,

Walter Bagehot

Mark Twain
1835–1910

Samuel Langhorne Clemens (Mark Twain), renowned American writer, lecturer and satirist, grew up in Hannibal, a Missouri port town on the Mississippi, the river that provided him with inspiration all his life. At fourteen, Clemens began working as a printer's apprentice, and also started writing his first pieces of journalism. He moved around the country a great deal, educating himself in libraries and working for various printers and publishers; at the age of twenty-two, he was inspired to become a steamboat pilot on the Mississippi, a dangerous and highly skilled occupation.

In 1868, Clemens fell in love with Olivia ('Livy') Langdon, the daughter of a family of wealthy liberals in upstate New York; her parents had been 'conductors' on the Underground Railroad for fugitive slaves. They were married in 1870.

Clemens was a very prolific and extremely success-ful writer of journalism, travel books and novels (*Tom Sawyer*, probably his most famous work, appeared in 1876), and travelled constantly on lecture tours around the US and Europe – he was enormously popular in the UK. On one of these tours, he met Charles Darwin, who was a huge admirer. Clemens was also an enthusiastic inventor; he registered several patents and poured hundreds of thousands of dollars into the development of the Paige typewriter, which astounded all who saw it but which never actually worked properly. He earned a good living but was hopeless with money, at one point declaring himself bankrupt.

He and Livy were very happily married and had four children; tragically, their first son died as a baby, and two of his daughters died in their twenties. Livy herself died in 1904, leaving her husband bereft.

To Livy on her thirtieth birthday
HARTFORD, *27 November 1875*

Livy darling,
Six years have gone by since I made my first great success in life and won you, and thirty years have passed since Providence made preparation for that happy success by sending you into the world. Every day we live together adds to the security of my confidence, that we can never any more wish to be separated than that we can ever imagine a regret that we were ever joined. You are dearer to me to-day, my child, than you were upon the last anniversary of this birth-day;

you were dearer then than you were a year before – you have grown more and more dear from the first of those anniversaries, and I do not doubt that this precious progression will continue on to the end.

Let us look forward to the coming anniversaries, with their age and their gray hairs without fear and without depression, trusting and believing that the love we bear each other will be sufficient to make them blessed.

So, with abounding affection for you and our babies, I hail this day that brings you the matronly grace and dignity of three decades!

Always Yours

S. L. C.

ST. NICHOLAS, *Aug. 26th, '78.*

Livy darling,

We came through a-whooping today, 6 hours tramp up steep hills and down steep hills, in mud and water shoe-deep, and in a steady pouring rain which never moderated a moment. I was as chipper and fresh as a lark all the way and arrived without the slightest sense of fatigue. But we were soaked and my shoes full of water, so we ate at once, stripped and went to bed for 2 ½ hours while our traps were thoroughly dried, and our boots greased in addition. Then we put our clothes on hot and went to table d'hote.

Made some nice English friends and shall see them at Zermatt tomorrow.

Gathered a small bouquet of new flowers, but they got spoiled. I sent you a safety-match box full of flowers last night from Leukerbad.

I have just telegraphed you to wire the family news to me at Riffel tomorrow. I do hope you are all well and having as jolly a time as we are, for I love you, sweetheart, and also, in a measure, the Bays [his small daughter's word for 'babies']. Give my love to Clara Spaulding and also to the cubs.

SAML.

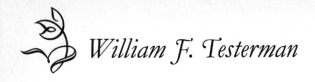

William F. Testerman

All that is known of William F. Testerman is that he was a first lieutenant in Company C of the 8th Tennessee Cavalry during the American Civil War.

To Miss Jane Davis
Gallotin, Tenn, 25 July 1864

Dear Miss,

I again take the opportunity of Droping you a few lines in answer to your kind letters which I received a few days ago one bearing date June '23' the other June the 24 it was a pleasure to me to have the honor to receive a letter from as charming a young girl as the one whos name was asscirbed at the bottom of each of them I was glad to hear that you was well but I was more glad to hear you express your mind as fully as what you did this note leaves me well and I truly hope that this will find you in good health I can't say anthing to you by letter more than what you have heard from my letters before + Jane I hope the time will soon come when I can get to see you again I can write many things to you but if I could see you I could tell you more in one minute than I can rite in aweek The letters that you wrote to me has proved verry satisfactory to meif you will stand up to what you told me in your letters I will be satisfied which I have no reasons to Doubt but what you will but if you was to fail it would almost break my heart for you are the girl that Iam Depending upon and if it was not for you I would not be riting by mycandle to night as you wrote to me that many miles seperated us in person if my heart was like yours we would be united in heart you kneed not to Dout Though we are fare apart at present my heart is with you everymoment for I often think of you when you are alseep when Travailing the lonesom roads in middle Tenn The thought of your sweet smiles is all the company I have I trust that you are cinsere in what you have wrote to me Your sparkling blue eys and rosey red cheeks has gaind my whole efections I hope for the time to come when we shall meet again then if you are in the notion that I am we can pass off the time in pleasure My time has come for sleep and I must soon close I want you to rite to me as soon as you can for I will be glad to hear from you any time Direct your letters as before and dont forget your best friends so I will end my few lines but mylove to you has no Endremember me as ever your love and friend. Excusebad riting.

William F. Testerman

Charles Stewart Parnell
1846–1891

Charles Stewart Parnell, 'the uncrowned king of Ireland', was an unlikely Irish nationalist. He was from landed Protestant gentry, his enthusiasms were hunting and cricket, and having been educated at Cambridge he had the manner and accent of an upper-class Englishman. He was initially a dreadfully shy and nervous public speaker; he was also very superstitious and had a deep aversion to the colour green — something of a problem given his line of work.

Parnell took his seat as a Home Rule MP in 1875. In 1880, at Westminster, he met Mrs Katharine O'Shea, the wife of a fellow Home Rule MP, and the two became lovers almost immediately.

Parnell was imprisoned in Kilmainham Gaol between October 1881 and May 1882, and the letter below dates from that time. Katharine was pregnant with his child, a daughter who was born that February but did not survive.

Katharine's husband, William O'Shea, turned a blind eye to his wife's adultery for ten years, possibly because she was set to inherit a large legacy from an aunt, and would be disinherited if there was a scandal. It seems unlikely that he did not know – Parnell had a cricket pitch laid out at the O'Shea house and established a study there, which must have given O'Shea some idea of what was going on. When the aunt died in 1890, however, he decided the situation was, after all, intolerable and filed for divorce, which was when the public scandal began. The case was a perfect storm of class, money, morality, sex and politics. Katharine was vilified as 'Kitty O'Shea' – 'Kitty' being slang for 'prostitute' – and the divorce ended Parnell's political career. The pair removed to Brighton, where they were married in June 1891; Parnell, whose constitution had always been fragile, died with his wife at his side less than four months later, at the age of forty-five.

To Katharine O'Shea,
Kilmainham, 14 October 1881

My Own Dearest Wifie,
I have found a means of communicating with you, and of your communicating in return.

Please put your letters into enclosed envelope, first putting them in an inner envelope, on the joining of which you can write your initials with a similar pencil to mine, and they will reach me all right. I am very comfortable here, and have a beautiful room facing the sun – the best in the prison. There are three or four of the best of the men in adjoining rooms with whom I can associate all day long, so that time does not hang heavy nor do I feel lonely. My only fear is about my darling Queenie. I have been racked with torture all today, last night, and yesterday, lest the shock may have hurt you or our child. Oh, darling, write or wire me as soon as you get this that you are well and will try not to be unhappy until you see your husband again. You may wire me here.

I have your beautiful face with me here; it is such a comfort. I kiss it every morning.

Your King

Oscar Wilde
1854–1900

Oscar Wilde was a playwright, novelist, essayist, critic, poet and wit. The effete poses of his youth and his dandyish appearance can still serve to mask his serious intellect: he studied at Trinity College, Dublin and Magdalen, Oxford, graduating with a double first in classics – not the achievement of someone who spent his time at university lolling about dispensing barbed witticisms. He believed in beauty – in dress and furnishings, certainly, but also in art and human relations. He is often written about as though his Irish nationality were basically an accident and to all intents and purposes he was an Englishman, but his sense of himself as Irish was strong, and politically, he was a supporter of Parnell.

Wilde married Constance Mary Lloyd, a Dublin Protestant, in 1884; she gave birth to two sons in quick succession. In 1891, Wilde met Lord Alfred Douglas, son of the Marquess of Queensberry. His subsequent love affair with 'Bosie' effectively ruined his life. In 1895, Douglas's father, famously aggressive, infuriated by his son's relationship with Wilde, left a card at Wilde's club inscribed 'To Oscar Wilde –

posing as Somdomite [sic]'. Wilde made the unwise decision to sue for libel. The case went to court but was abandoned. The vindictive Marquess pursued Wilde through the office of the public prosecutor, which resulted in his standing trial on various counts of gross indecency. He was found guilty and sentenced to two years' hard labour; he served his sentence at Pentonville and then at Reading.

Wilde left prison physically and psychologically destroyed. Popular belief has it that he was abandoned by Douglas, but in fact, Lord Alfred wrote letters to the newspapers protesting the sentence, and petitioned the Queen for clemency. On his release, Wilde drifted from place to place (Constance had not divorced him, but had moved away, and changed her and the childrens' surname), frequently meeting up with Douglas. He died in a Paris hotel room in 1900, declaring a few days beforehand, 'My wallpaper and I are fighting a duel to the death. One or other of us has to go.'

To Lord Alfred Douglas, March 1893
Sent from the Savoy Hotel, London

Dearest of all Boys,
Your letter was delightful, red and yellow wine to me; but I

am sad and out of sorts. Bosie, you must not make scenes with me. They kill me, they wreck the loveliness of life. I cannot see you, so Greek and gracious, distorted with passion. I cannot listen to your curved lips saying hideous things to me. I would sooner be blackmailed by every renter in London than have you bitter, unjust, hating. I must see you soon. You are the divine thing I want, the thing of grace and beauty; but I don't know how to do it. Shall I come to Salisbury? My bill here is £49 for a week. I have also got a new sitting-room over the Thames. Why are you not here, my dear, my wonderful boy? I fear I must leave, no money, no credit, and a heart of lead.

Your own Oscar

To Lord Alfred Douglas
Sent from Courtfield Gardens, 20 May 1895

My child,
Today it was asked to have the verdicts rendered separately. Taylor is probably being judged at this moment, so that I have been able to come back here. My sweet rose, my delicate flower, my lily of lilies, it is perhaps in prison that I am going to test the power of love. I am going to see if I cannot make the bitter warders sweet by the intensity of the love I bear you. I have had moments when I thought it would be wiser to separate. Ah! moments of weakness and madness! Now I see that that would have mutilated my life, ruined my art, broken the musical chords which make

a perfect soul. Even covered with mud I shall praise you, from the deepest abysses I shall cry to you. In my solitude you will be with me. I am determined not to revolt but to accept every outrage through devotion to love, to let my body be dishonoured so long as my soul may always keep the image of you. From your silken hair to your delicate feet you are perfection to me. Pleasure hides love from us, but pain reveals it in its essence. O dearest of created things, if someone wounded by silence and solitude comes to you, dishonoured, a laughing-stock, Oh! you can close his wounds by touching them and restore his soul which unhappiness had for a moment smothered. Nothing will be difficult for you then, and remember, it is that hope which makes me live, and that hope alone. What wisdom is to the philosopher, what God is to his saint, you are to me. To keep you in my soul, such is the goal of this pain which men call life. O my love, you whom I cherish above all things, white narcissus in an unmown field, think of the burden which falls to you, a burden which love alone can make light. But be not saddened by that, rather be happy to have filled with an immortal love the soul of a man who now weeps in hell, and yet carries heaven in his heart. I love you, I love you, my heart is a rose which your love has brought to bloom, my life is a desert fanned by the delicious breeze of your breath, and whose cool spring are your eyes; the imprint of your little feet makes valleys of shade for me, the odour of your hair is like myrrh, and wherever you go you exhale the perfumes of the cassia tree.

Love me always, love me always. You have been the supreme, the perfect love of my life; there can be no other.

I decided that it was nobler and more beautiful to stay. We could not have been together. I did not want to be called a coward or a deserter. A false name, a disguise, a hunted life, all that is not for me, to whom you have been revealed on that high hill where beautiful things are transfigured.

O sweetest of all boys, most loved of all loves, my soul clings to your soul, my life is your life, and in all the world of pain and pleasure you are my ideal of admiration and joy.

Oscar

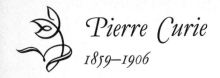

Pierre Curie
1859–1906

When Pierre Curie met Marie Sklodovska at the Sorbonne in 1894, she was a penniless student from Poland. Marie was twenty-four when she arrived in Paris. Despite having no money, and having to pursue her studies in a language in which she was far from fluent, Marie took her mathematics degree at the head of her class in 1893, and her physics degree second in her class a year later.

Pierre had already established himself as a brilliant physicist when the two of them met; what they shared was a fierce idealism, an almost terrifying single-mindedness and a complete lack of interest in plaudits or status. The letter here was written about a year before they married; Marie had been intending to return to Poland, and Pierre is clearly trying, in a very shy and endearing way, to persuade her that they should be together.

The Curies' relationship was quite extraordinarily productive. Working together in a tiny shed, they discovered two new elements, radium and polonium (the latter named for Marie's country of birth), and were awarded half the Nobel Prize in Physics in 1903.

Tragedy struck in 1906, when Pierre was run over and killed by a horse-drawn carriage in Paris. Marie, left with two young daughters, was grief-stricken, but her strength of purpose saw her through, and in 1908, she was appointed the first ever female professor at the Sorbonne; in 1911 she was awarded the Nobel Prize in Chemistry.

Both Marie and Pierre displayed signs of radiation sickness during their lifetime – Pierre liked to carry a sample of radium in his waistcoat pocket to show people, and Marie kept radium salt by her bed that shone in the darkness. Marie died of leukaemia in 1934 and was the first woman to be buried in the Pantheon in Paris. The papers the Curies left behind give off significant radiation, and scholars today wishing to look at their notebooks in the Bibliothèque Nationale must first sign a waiver.

To Marie Sklodovska, 10 August 1894

Nothing could have given me greater pleasure than to get news of you. The prospect of remaining two months without hearing about you had been extremely disagreeable to me: that is to say, your little note was more than welcome.

I hope you are laying up a stock of good air and that you

will come back to us in October. As for me, I think I shall not go anywhere; I shall stay in the country, where I spend the whole day in front of my open window or in the garden.

We have promised each other – haven't we? – to be at least great friends. If you will only not change your mind! For there are no promises that are binding; such things cannot be ordered at will. It would be a fine thing, just the same, in which I hardly dare believe, to pass our lives near each other, hypnotized by our dreams: *your* patriotic dreams, *our* humanitarian dream, and *our* scientific dream.

Of all those dreams the last is, I believe, the only legitimate one. I mean by that we are powerless to change the social order and, even if we were not, we should not know what to do; in taking action, no matter in what direction, we should never be sure of not doing more harm than good, by retarding some inevitable evolution. From the scientific point of view, on the contrary, we may hope to do something; the ground is solider here, and any discovery that we may make, however small, will remain acquired knowledge.

See how it works out: it is agreed that we shall be great friends, but if you leave France in a year it would be an altogether too Platonic friendship, that of two creatures who would never see each other again. Wouldn't it be better for you to stay with me? I know that this question angers you, and that you don't want to speak of it again – and then, too, I feel so thoroughly unworthy of you from every point of view.

I thought of asking your permission to meet you *by chance* in Freibourg. But you are staying there, unless I am mistaken, only one day, and on that day you will of course belong to our friends the Kovalskis.

Believe me your very devoted

Pierre Curie

I should be happy if you would write to me and give me the assurance that you intend to come back in October. If you write direct to Sceaux the letters would get to me quicker: Pierre Curie, 13 rue des Sablons, Sceaux (Seine).

G. K. Chesterton
1874–1936

Gilbert Keith Chesterton is not widely read today, and is probably best known for his 'Father Brown' detective stories, but during his lifetime he was a bestselling novelist, a noted wit and a literary celebrity. He had a formidable intellect but a wayward mind; he attended art school and flirted with the idea of a political career, but it was only when he began writing journalism for the thriving magazine and newspaper market of 1890s London that he found his place in the world.

Chesterton as a boy and young man had no interest in religion, but as he reached his twenties he was increasingly attracted to Christianity. He met Frances Blogg, the daughter of a diamond merchant of French descent, in 1896, and her devout Anglo-Catholicism informed his own religious beliefs. His letter to her below is a model of charm, self-deprecation, wit and affection. They were married in 1901.

It was in the years leading up to the Great War that Chesterton's fame was at its height. He certainly cut an arresting figure; vast (six foot four) and vastly overweight, he habitually wore a cloak and a broad-brimmed hat, and was a fixture in the public houses around Fleet Street. (A famous anecdote has him telling his friend George Bernard Shaw, 'To look at you, anyone would think there was a famine in England,' to which Shaw replied, 'To look at you, anyone would think you caused it.')

In 1909, Frances decided that he needed to be removed from London and its temptations, and they moved to Beaconsfield in Buckinghamshire. Their marriage was happy, although their not having children was a source of sadness to both.

Chesterton's post-war writing was increasingly religious and mystical, and he finally converted to Catholicism in 1922. His work was disfigured by anti-Semitism, and while his admirers have made the case that it was variously 1) not that extreme and 2) part and parcel of the time in which he lived, the accusation cannot be dismissed. He died in 1936 at home in Beaconsfield; Frances survived him.

To Frances Blogg (189–?)

. . . I am looking over the sea and endeavouring to reckon up the estate I have to offer you. As far as I can make out my equipment for starting on a journey to fairyland consists of the following items.

1st. A Straw Hat. The oldest part of this admirable relic shows traces of pure Norman work. The vandalism of Cromwell's soldiers has left us little of the original hat-band.

2nd. A Walking Stick, very knobby and heavy: admirably fitted to break the head of any denizen of Suffolk who denies that you are the noblest of ladies, but of no other manifest use.

3rd. A copy of Walt Whitman's poems, once nearly given to Salter, but quite forgotten. It has his name in it still with an affectionate inscription from his sincere friend Gilbert Chesterton. I wonder if he will ever have it.

4th. A number of letters from a young lady, containing everything good and generous and loyal and holy and wise that isn't in Walt Whitman's poems.

5th. An unwieldy sort of a pocket knife, the blades mostly having an edge of a more varied and picturesque outline than is provided by the prosaic cutler. The chief element however is a thing 'to take the stones out of a horse's hoof'. What a beautiful sensation of security it gives one to reflect that if one should ever have money enough to buy a horse and should happen to have a stone in his hoof – that one is ready; one stands prepared, with a defiant smile!

6th. Passing from the last miracle of practical foresight, we come to a box of matches. Every now and then I strike one of these, because fire is beautiful and burns your fingers. Some people think this a waste of matches: the same people who object to the building of Cathedrals.

7th. About three pounds in gold and silver, the remains

of one of Mr Unwin's bursts of affection: those explosions of spontaneous love for myself, which, such is the perfect order and harmony of his mind, occur at startlingly exact intervals of time.

8th. A book of Children's Rhymes, in manuscript, called 'Weather Book' about ? finished, and destined for Mr Nutt. I have been working at it fairly steadily, which I think jolly creditable under the circumstances. One can't put anything interesting in it. They'll understand those things when they grow up.

9th. A tennis racket – nay, start not. It is a part of the new regime, and the only new and neat-looking thing in the Museum. We'll soon mellow it – like the straw hat. My brother and I are teaching each other lawn tennis.

10th. A soul, hitherto idle and omnivorous but now happy enough to be ashamed of itself.

11th. A body, equally idle and quite equally omnivorous, absorbing tea, coffee, claret, sea-water and oxygen to its own perfect satisfaction. It is happiest swimming, I think, the sea being a convenient size.

12th. A Heart – mislaid somewhere. And that is about all the property of which an inventory can be made at present. After all, my tastes are stoically simple. A straw hat, a stick, a box of matches and some of his own poetry. What more does man require?

Letters from the Great War

Captain Alfred Bland

Written while serving in France with the 22nd Battalion of the Manchester Regiment, to his wife Violet. Bland was killed on 1 July 1916, the first day of the Battle of the Somme.

To Violet

My only and eternal blessedness,

I wonder whether you resent my cheerfulness ever! Do you, dear? Because you might, you know. I ought, by the rules of love, to spend my days and nights in an eternity of sighs and sorrow for our enforced parting. And by all the rules of war, I ought to be enduring cold and hardship, hunger and fatigue, bitterness of soul and dismay of heart.

Alas! What shall I say in my defence? Because not even Merriman can depress me, and as for the CO, I am simply impertinent to him, while the dull routine of being behind the line fills me with an inexhaustible supply of cheerful patience. What shall we say about it? Would it rejoice you if I confessed to being utterly miserable every now and then? If I told you how I loathed war and hated every minute that prolonged it? If I admitted that I yearn hourly for my return, my final return away from it all? If I said that

I hated my brother officers and was sick of the sight of the Company? If I described the filthy squalor of the village streets, the sickening repetition of low clouds and sulky drizzle and heavy rain, and the dreary monotony of ration beef and ration bread? Would you be glad or sorry?

Oh, I know how sympathetic and sad you would feel, and I know you would not be glad at all. Would you? And if you were glad, you would be all wrong; because, even if those things were true, it wouldn't bring us together again, it wouldn't make me love you more, it wouldn't sweeten those embraces we are deprived of for the moment, it wouldn't strengthen our divine oneness one scrap. Would it?

No, my darling, thank the heavens daily that in all circumstances you will be right in picturing your boy out here simply brimming over with gaiety irrepressible. I am becoming a byword. Cushion says, 'I like you, Bill Bland.' Why? Because I am always laughing with everybody and everything, greeting the seen and the unseen with a cheer. And it isn't a pose. It's the solemn truth.

So let us go back again to those imaginary admissions above. I am never utterly miserable, not even when I yearn most for the touch of your lips and a sight of my boys. Why? Because I am in France, where the war is, and I know I ought to be here. And I don't loathe war, I love ninety-five per cent of it, and hate the thought of it being ended too soon. And I don't yearn hourly for my final return, although I am very pleasantly excited at the possibility of nine days' leave in March, which indeed we haven't earned by any means so far.

And I don't loathe my brother officers but love them more than I dreamed possible, and as for my Company, why bless it! And the mud is such friendly mud, somehow, so yielding and considerate – and I don't have to clean my own boots. And I have lost the habit of regarding the weather, for if it rains, we get wet, and if it doesn't, we don't, and if the sun shines, how nice! And as for our food, well, I've given you an idea of that before, and I have nothing to add to the statements made in this House on November 30 and December 6 last or any other time.

No, dear, whether you like it or not, I am fundamentally happy and on the surface childishly gay. And there's an end on't.

Post just going.

Good night, darling.

Ever your

Alfred

Regimental Sergeant-Major James Milne

James 'Jim' Milne was a company sergeant-major who served with the 4th Battalion, Gordon Highlanders. The following is a farewell letter to his wife Meg, in the event of his being killed in battle.

Milne came through the war, and returned home to Scotland.

My own beloved wife,

I do not know how to start this letter. The circumstances are different from any under which I ever wrote before. I am not to post it but will leave it in my pocket, and if anything happens to me, someone will perhaps post it. We are going over the top this forenoon and only God in Heaven knows who will come out of it alive. I am going into it now, Dearest, sure that I am in His hands and that whatever happens, I look to Him, in this world and the world to come.

If I am called, my regret is that I leave you and my Bairns, but I leave you all to His great mercy and goodness, knowing that He will look over you all and watch you. I trust in Him to bring me through, but should He decree otherwise then though we do not know His reasons, we know it must be best. I go to Him with your dear face the last vision on earth I shall see and your name upon my lips. You, the best of Women. You will look after my Darling Bairns for me and tell them how their Daddy died.

Oh! How I love you all, and as I sit here waiting I wonder what you are doing at home. I must not do that. It is hard enough sitting waiting. We may move at any minute. When this reaches you, for me there will be no more war – only eternal peace and waiting for you.

You must be brave, my Darling, for my sake, for I leave you the Bairns. It is a legacy of struggle for you, but God will look after you and we shall meet again when there will be no more parting. I am to write no more, Sweetheart. I know you will read my old letters and keep them for my sake, and that you will love me or my memory till we meet again.

May God in his Mercy look over you and bless you all till that day we shall met again in His own Good time. May He in that same Mercy preserve me today.

GoodBye Meg,

Eternal love from

Yours for Ever and Ever,

Jim

Second Lieutenant John Lindsay Rapoport

John Rapoport, aged twenty-four, became engaged during the spring of 1918; the letter below is to his fiancée. At the beginning of June, he was posted missing during the third battle of the Aisne. His body was never recovered.

6 May 1918

The mail has just come in and I've got fourteen letters! Among them, my darling, were five from you. So you can imagine what I feel like. I got the very first one of all tonight, the one you sent to me at Havre. They've been awfully slack in forwarding it.

Darling, you were just splendid when you saw me off at Waterloo. You just typified the women of England by your attitude, everything for us men, and you have your dark times to yourselves so as not to depress us . . .

You mean so much to me, you have no idea how much. Life without you would be absolutely empty. I wonder however I got on before. As a matter of fact, I am full of love and for the last two or three years I've had a longing to pour it out on someone, and I've always lived in the hope of doing so – that kept me going. Now I've got someone on whom I can and have lavished all my love.

My darling, I love and adore you from the bottom of my heart. You wait till I come home – you will get some kisses then, and I shall hold you tight – you know how, my darling, don't you?

I am so glad we are both alike on the question of friends. Of course I want you to carry on with your men friends just as if I didn't exist. One thing I am [as] sure of as that I exist: that is that I have all your heart and all your love. So I just want you to enjoy yourself – I love you so much. Have a topping time on the river and at shows, etc, with your friends, won't you?

I asked WW to write to me still, though we were engaged – just as friends. I feel very sorry for your friends. Just impress on them that you can be chums just as before. I know it isn't quite the same, but I should like it, because I know what a help you'd be to any man. Just thank your friends for their good wishes, will you?

Oh, the more I think of it, the more I realize how lucky I am in having you for my *own* darling wife-to-be. Oh, hasn't God been good to me – far more than I deserve.

The following sources were invaluable:

Love in Letters Illustrated in the Correspondence of Eminent Persons with Biographical Sketches of the Writers by Allan Grant, G. W. Carleton & Co., New York 1867

Love Letters of Famous Men and Women, J. T. Merydew (ed.), Remington & Co., London 1888

Love Affairs of Famous Men & Women, Henri Pène du Bois (ed.), Gibbings & Company, London 1900

The Letters of Robert Browning and Elizabeth Barrett Browning, Smith, Elder & Co., London, 1900

Love Letters of Famous People, Freeman Bunting (ed.), Gay and Bird, London, 1907

Letters of Love, Arthur L. Humphreys, London 1911

Love Letters of Great Men and Women, C. H. Charles (ed.), Stanley Paul & Co, London, 1924

The Love Letters of Robert Burns and Clarinda, Donny O'Rourke (ed.), based on 1843 edition, edited by W. C. M'Lehose

Mark Twain's Letters, edited and with a commentary by Albert Bigelow Paine, Harper & Brothers Publishers, New York, 1917

Love Letters, Antonia Fraser (ed.), Weidenfeld & Nicolson, London, 1976

Love Letters, Peter Washington (ed.), Everyman's Library, 1996

Dispatches from the Heart: Love Letters from the Front Line, Jamie Ambrose (ed.), Little Books Ltd, London, 2005

Acknowledgements

Thanks to JG for the idea, JB for commissioning it, RM for letting him, FC, KT, WD and IA for making it look lovely, and to all my friends at Pan Macmillan. Thanks to the staff at the British Library. Thanks to my family. Heartfelt thanks to DP.

A note on the type

This book is set in Monotype Garamond, an old-style serif typeface prized for its consistency and fluency. The original 'Garamond' was the work of the fifteenth-century punch-cutter Claude Garamond, whose lower-case letters were in turn inspired by the handwriting of Angelo Vergecio, librarian to King Francis I of France. A twentieth-century vogue for recutting historical typefaces lead to a rash of 'Garamond' letterforms, from Stempel Garamond to Granjon and Sabon. In 1926, however, it was revealed that other new members of the Garamond 'family', such as Monotype Garamond, were actually based on the work of a later punch-cutter called Jean Jannon.